Praise for *How to Get* *(Without Really D*

"Many people have had near-death experiences and have strong messages for the rest of us. Robert Kopecky's reflections are unusually intelligent and presented in a lively mix of humor and seriousness. I had fun reading this book and appreciated Robert's fresh way of offering traditional wisdom."

—Thomas Moore, author of *Care of the Soul* and *Ageless Soul*

"In this book, age-old questions are answered by Kopecky as to why many people have different NDE experiences. Returning from the brink of death, he also speaks of three important truths which when demonstrated are liberating and healing. Helping us to engage with life, these truths will lead us on a transformational journey in finding a life filled with joy while creating Heaven on Earth."

—Anita Moorjani, *New York Times* bestselling author of *Dying to Be Me* and *What if This Is Heaven?*

"I appreciate and endorse Robert's key themes, which are presented with engaging and heartfelt first-person examples: if we seek peace of mind in this life, we'll find it through acts of kindness, humility, honesty, forgiveness, compassion, and service. These practices are universal, but are often expressed in a dogmatic fashion, rather than in the friendly manner found in this book. Perhaps his clarity boils down to the adage 'Religion is for people who're afraid of going to hell. Spirituality is for those who've already been there.'"

—Josh Korda, author and guiding teacher of Dharma Punx NYC

"Robert Kopecky's latest book flows with a humble power of perception and passion. The wisdom and insights in his words are filled with a gentle brilliance. The holy trinity of perspective, presence, and purpose give us the what, how, and why of life in this physical universe and in our lives beyond. His wonderful exercises bring the afterlife bliss into our daily living. His tips on prayer and meditation offer us excellent guidance to inner peace."

—Brother Edward Salisbury, DDiv, FD, hospice minister and multiple NDE survivor

"Intriguing and captivating, *How to Get to Heaven (Without Really Dying)* offers a new perspective on the topic of near-death experiences. Possibly the most insightful book on how to obtain the enlightenment experienced by those who have gone through a NDE, *How to Get to Heaven (Without Really Dying)* offers hope and encouragement to experience lasting change."
—Marianne Pestana, host of *Moments with Marianne* at iHeart Radio

"A landscape of love is all around us and yet mysteriously hidden. Based on his own near-death experiences, Robert Kopecky gives us keys to this landscape. Practicing the simple qualities of kindness, compassion, humility, and service open us to the love, light, and magic of life. Heaven is not 'somewhere else' but is a state in which we are reconnected to the Divine Consciousness that is within and all around us. This beautiful book helps us to live in this miraculous realm, awake in its wonder."
—Llewellyn Vaughan-Lee, PhD, author of
Sufism: The Transformation of the Heart

"Robert Kopecky clearly identifies techniques to help stop our de-evolution of society by remembering our true purpose—to be of service to others. He resurrects the value of old texts which have guidance…The truth has been with us all along and Robert helps by reminding us of what we already know, and how to put it into practice."
—Linda P. Truax, Board Secretary of the International
Association for Near-Death Studies

"Robert Kopecky has a gift for asking eternal questions and distilling the answers into bite-sized pieces of wisdom gleaned from his own life experience. His ability to grapple with the big questions in an authentic and humorous way renders them more accessible to those of us curious about the deeper meaning of existence."
—Jerilyn Hesse, Programs Manager at the Esalen Institute

"*How to Get to Heaven (Without Really Dying)* is an excellent resource. Not only does Kopecky explain how meditation can enable us to access a unique channel of consciousness that could be referred to as 'Heaven'…he states, 'Fear is not real, unless you concede to give it that power,' and successfully illustrates that statement and others by covering topics such as kindness, honesty, forgiveness, and of course, meditation."
—TheMindfulWord.org

HOW TO GET TO HEAVEN

HEAVEN

(WITHOUT REALLY DYING)

About the Author

Robert Kopecky is a California-born writer, artist, and speaker (from Brooklyn, NY) who lived a variety of lives until becoming an award-winning illustrator, art director, and animation designer. In the course of his unusual path, he survived three dramatically different Near Death Experiences that inspired years of study and meditation and led to the publication of his book *How to Survive Life (and Death)*. He explores, writes, and teaches about the lessons he learned "the hard way," and blogs at The Mindful Word, Gaia.com, Soul Life Times, and other places around the web. Visit him online at RobertKopecky .blogspot.com.

HOW TO GET TO HEAVEN

(WITHOUT REALLY DYING)

WISDOM FROM A NEAR DEATH SURVIVOR

ROBERT KOPECKY

Llewellyn Publications
Woodbury, Minnesota

First Edition
First Printing, 2018

Cover illustration by Robert Kopecky

The Soul of Rumi by Coleman Barks used with permission

Llewellyn Publications is a registered trademark of Llewellyn Worldwide Ltd.

Library of Congress Cataloging-in-Publication Data
  Names: Kopecky, Robert, author.
  Title: How to get to heaven (without really dying) : wisdom from a near death survivor / by Robert Kopecky.
  Description: First Edition. | Woodbury : Llewellyn Worldwide, Ltd., 2018. | Includes bibliographical references and index.
  Identifiers: LCCN 2017052908 (print) | LCCN 2017058801 (ebook) | ISBN 9780738755489 (ebook) | ISBN 9780738753218 (alk. paper)
  Subjects: LCSH: Future life. | Heaven. | Near-death experiences—Religious aspects. | Conduct of life.
  Classification: LCC BL535 (ebook) | LCC BL535 .K67 2018 (print) | DDC 202/.3—dc23
  LC record available at https://lccn.loc.gov/2017052908

Llewellyn Worldwide Ltd. does not participate in, endorse, or have any authority or responsibility concerning private business transactions between our authors and the public.
  All mail addressed to the author is forwarded but the publisher cannot, unless specifically instructed by the author, give out an address or phone number.
  Any Internet references contained in this work are current at publication time, but the publisher cannot guarantee that a specific location will continue to be maintained. Please refer to the publisher's website for links to authors' websites and other sources.

Llewellyn Publications
A Division of Llewellyn Worldwide Ltd.
2143 Wooddale Drive
Woodbury, MN 55125-2989
www.llewellyn.com

Printed in the United States of America

Other Books by Robert Kopecky

How to Survive Life (and Death):
A Guide for Happiness in This World and Beyond
(Conari Press, 2014)

Contents

Exercises ... xi

Introduction: Finding Heaven (the Easier Way) ... 1

PART I: PERSPECTIVE

Chapter 1: Gaining Perspective Through Simple Principles:
Cultivating a View from on High ... 15

Chapter 2: Kindness: It's Very Nice to Be Very Kind ... 25

Chapter 3: Humility: How a Humble Life
Is So Totally Fabulous ... 35

Chapter 4: Honesty: The Gift of Honesty Is Really No Lie ... 47

Chapter 5: Forgiveness: It's For Giving ... and For Getting ... 55

Chapter 6: Compassion: Becoming a
Passionate Compassionate ... 63

Chapter 7: Service: How You Really Can
Meet the Nicest People ... 75

PART II: PRESENCE

Chapter 8: Finding Presence Now:
It's Always Been Now, and Always Will Be ... 87

Chapter 9: The Presence That Lasts:
Uncovering Ancient Paths to Heaven ... 103

PART III: PURPOSE

Chapter 10: Discovering Divine Purpose
Through Personal Actions:
Becoming a Heavenly Human Being ... 129

Chapter 11: Looking into the Truth: Turning from Our Dark
Corners to Face the Light ... 139

Chapter 12: Meditation Works When Your Mind Doesn't:
Don't Just Do Something—Sit There! ... 151

Chapter 13: Recognize the Sacred in Everything:
... and (Surprise!) Become a Whole Lot Happier ... 171

Chapter 14: Look for the Divine in Others:
Realizing Heavenly Relationships ... 181

Chapter 15: Create a Divine World:
Making This Place Look More Like Paradise ... 195

Conclusion: The Everyday Realization of Heaven ... 209

Appendix: Many Heavens to Live, Many Ways to Die:
Why We Really (Don't) Die ... 213

Bibliography and Interdimensional Reading List ... 217

Acknowledgments ... 223

Index ... 225

Exercises

Rising above the Ego ... 19

Ways of Discovering Real Kindness ... 32

Ways of Celebrating Real Humility ... 44

Ways of Uncovering Real Honesty ... 53

Ways of Releasing Real Forgiveness ... 60

Ways of Opening to Real Compassion ... 73

Ways to Discover the Real Value of Service ... 83

Entering into Presence ... 101

Reading Into the Ancient Now ... 125

Finding Your Purpose Finder ... 138

Teach Your Eyes to Look for Love ... 150

Guiding Yourself to Bliss ... 169

Recognize the Sacred in Everything ... 179

Have an Open-Hearted Day ... 193

Twenty Tips for Living in Heaven ... 201

Introduction:
Finding Heaven (the Easier Way)

Everyone wants to go to Heaven, and it seems that a few of us—including yours truly—may have briefly visited there already. There's no qualification for claiming knowledge of the afterlife equivalent to surviving what's commonly called a Near Death Experience, shortened to the familiar acronym *NDE*. As unlikely as it may sound (even to me), over the course of fifteen years I happen to have survived *three of them*. I lived through three very different Near Death Experiences at three very different times of my life. You could say, in a funny way, that I got lucky.

I obviously overdid it a little, and while I would never recommend multiple Near Death Experiences as a means to realizing the amazing spiritual truths at work in our lives and our world, eventually it did work for me—in profound and mysterious ways. Unfortunately, it required some forceful knockings (mostly with my head) on doors leading into a different, magical reality. Those lessons were painful but, needless to say, intensely educational. It's my aim to pass those lessons along to you in an easier, more enjoyable way—so please just follow my suggestions (and not my example) when I say that you don't have to actually die to go to Heaven. There are definitely much better ways to find that elusive realm of serenity and wonder right here and now, many of which we'll be exploring in the pages of this book.

While my case is obviously unusual, I'm not at all alone in my experience of life after death. Thousands if not millions of people have been on the other side of this mortal veil by now and lived to tell about it. Clinical studies and polls suggest that approximately 5 to 15 percent of people who die and "come back to life" report experiencing a conscious reality existing beyond this one. [1, 2, 3]

Some of the afterworlds they describe are classically Heaven-like, replete with the grandeur of angelic choirs, winged entities, and ascendant beings of light; while others are dark and definitively hellish, full of fire, brimstone, sharp-toothed demons (with pitchforks even)—all that kind of scary, sinister stuff. The majority of these very personal experiences unfold somewhere in the middle, simple and humble NDEs that aren't nearly as imaginative as those more spectacular experiences—more like normal life as we all know it. Aside from the inherently surreal circumstances of my NDEs, mine were more "normal" that way. They were like this life, only different. Like this life, they took place in a potentially magical world where practically anything could potentially happen.

I believe that all of those different NDE stories are the truthful experiences of every one of those experiencers, but just where do the differences in their stories (as in mine) come from? Why does the afterlife seem to be configured differently for different people? Perhaps the answer to these differing experiences of Heaven can be found by looking at our personal earthly experiences—the nature of our *perspective* on life (the way we look at it), the *presence* we bring to living (how we live it), and the roles our individual and collective *purpose* has given us to play (the reason why we're here).

These three themes will be our focus as we move forward together in this book.

The Location of Heaven

I'd describe my three "near deaths" as having sent me into different powerful *states of being*, as well as to apparently different locations.

---

1. Knoblauch et al., "Different Kinds of Near-Death Experience," *Journal of Near-Death Studies.*

2. Van Lommel et al., "Near-Death Experience in Survivors of Cardiac Arrest," *Lancet.*

3. Poll results in Gallup and Proctor, *Adventures in Immortality.*

They were more sensory *here-and-now* experiences than physical journeys off to specific destinations. So, while keeping some of those traditional ideals in mind, I'll be discussing and describing Heaven in terms of those states of being—experiences of light, sensation, and potential (in this earthly life or in lives to follow) rather than as any single, actual location we may eventually arrive at.

Lots of NDEs, as different survivors attest, are very similar to one another, and follow familiar motifs, like seeing one's own lifeless body from above, traveling down a tunnel toward a light at the end of it, meeting one's relatives in a radiantly lit field, having a life review, or actually meeting God in one form or another. Many of them don't at all resemble the classic concepts of Heaven as featured in religious illustrations, while others do. What they do all hold in common is that peek into a highly personalized realm of wondrous possibility: the expansive visions of a place of Love and light, where the continuation of life carries the promise of joyful realization, and where bliss isn't luckily discovered in little bits here and there but instead is the regular condition of being.

Of the three NDEs that I experienced, all of them fit into one of those classic motifs, yet like so many afterlife experiences, each was entirely different from the others—save one thing: no matter the differing circumstances of each, I never exited the realm of *Consciousness* in any of them. That is to say, I never felt like I was not *myself*, or in some way disconnected from the experience of living—it just wasn't *this* life. I was always conscious, but I experienced my own consciousness in a very different way than I typically do in this world. Perhaps I was experiencing a completely different world of *Divine Consciousness*—an unbounded world without limitations—absolutely connected and cared for, intuitively empathetic, and wrapped in Love. That's the heavenly experience that doesn't rely on any location or on supernatural capabilities; it was just that *sensation*, that profound knowledge of Love and a constant divine connection, alive within an inexpressible, expansive quality of Consciousness. *That* was where Heaven was, where it always is, and I believe where it can always reliably be found, if we know how to look for it.

So what does account for the differences in all of these experiencers' different Near Death Experiences? What does it take for some folks to really "go to Heaven," while others (like me, in one of them) have less-than-heavenly experiences? I think those answers are present anytime you take a look around this world we live in—you'll see all the same underlying mechanisms of our spiritual existence at work in each and every instant, often right in plain sight, in any world we occupy.

To begin with, many of us are born into a kind of Heaven or Hell right *here*, in our life on this Earth. We can be dropped into desperately violent and hopeless situations, or may awaken to a life where just about every heavenly option and opportunity imaginable is already given to us. All of us have known people who've been raised in pretty hellish situations, who then magically grow gardens of happiness and fulfillment out of the least likely plot of ground; while others are born into very rich soil, but seem to find themselves hopelessly locked out of the garden—forever banging on the door to get back in. So the question is: Who ultimately experiences that heavenly state of being, and how did they go about getting there?

It's not my job to describe the model landscape or architecture of Heaven to anyone, or to give you expectations about what you may or may not see and meet on the other side. That would be like trying to describe my life to you as if it were going to be exactly like your own. What I am able to give you—what I do know of Heaven—lives in the landscape and architecture of the human heart. The lessons I have to give are those that have slowly grown out of the periodically unforgiving ground of Life (and death), mixed with a deep longing to return to that place of Love and joy—once and forever.

Besides, even with my three NDEs, I never met Saint Peter, or saw a tunnel with the light at the end, or met my granddad in that meadow, or had a face-to-face with God. For me, it had less to do with where I went and what I saw than with how it made me feel.

In that way, I know I can experience Heaven or Hell from wherever I currently stand.

The distance we imagine between our selves and our aspirations is mostly an illusion. The trip itself can be deceptively short—often it's just the distance from our head to our heart. It's a journey you won't need to pack anything for—in fact, you'll only need to *unpack* a few very important necessities, namely your willingness, your curiosity, and your imagination. Don't worry about having enough faith to bring with you—we'll find plenty of that along the way.

So how do we go about finding our way to a place that isn't one specific location—or seems to require a facility for extra-dimensional travel to get there? Let's start by putting aside ideas about landscapes and architecture, and concentrate on its environment and atmosphere. Let's begin by concentrating on the way Heaven will *feel*.

When we think of Heaven, we think of a place where a sense of grace prevails, where the energy around us contributes to a seamless sensation of comfort and joy. All the elements of an easy existence—carrying a clear conscience; a sense of physical lightness; an effortless, open-hearted acceptance of everyone and everything; an instinctive impulse for empathy and fellowship; a flow of positive direction and a meaningful "calling"—all of this and more is enfolded in that imaginary atmosphere, in the atmosphere of *Love* (which we know is not imaginary).

By all of this I don't mean that Heaven will never be a real physical place, but that it will always be located in the eternal moment where your soul chooses to reside right *now*—where you choose to live in your heart. Going to Heaven isn't exclusively the result of physically dying from this amazing yet unavoidably difficult world. Going to Heaven (now or later) is always the result of *how we engage ourselves in the eternal field of Divine Consciousness*.

Lessons from My Near Death Experiences

In my three excursions to "the other side," I brought back three very important lessons that I'd like to frame our adventures to Heaven in. These are lessons of perspective, presence, and purpose. They'll serve as a starting point for our excursion through the simple principles, age-old wisdom, and personal actions that can open up the proper passages for us to follow. This is where you can save yourself a lot of my bumps and bruises, because these lessons are available to us *here and now*, on the proper side of the curtain, so to speak. I had to learn them the hard way for emphasis, I suppose.

1) The Lesson of Perspective

In my first NDE I was in a single-car accident, while fussing with a broken cassette tape deck (that'll date me), driving along an unfamiliar stretch of road at sundown. Distracted, I clipped the side of an oddly parked car, sending me straight into a telephone pole. The next instant, I found myself at the top of the utility pole, looking down onto the accident scene below. I witnessed myself—my body—hanging partially out of the driver's side window of the smashed car, and saw porch lights popping on and the neighbors running out to the crash, and then the ambulance arriving and loading up my unconscious body. I tried to talk to the little gathering of onlookers, but no one seemed able to see or hear me, at least no one acknowledged me. I seemed to be dimensionally *dislocated*. Strangely enough, I felt really, really good—in fact, I felt *wonderful*, but clearly I was no longer in my body, or in any body, for that matter.

After a bit I was shepherded off to a rather heavenly place—my first experience of "the Sweet Hereafter"—that was pastoral and beautifully park-like. I underwent a very pleasant kind of interview there, the experience of which seems vivid but the details too indistinct to report reliably. When I woke up, some eighteen hours later, one understanding filled me—and this is the basis of my first lesson: "You" are not only your body. I know it feels like it most of the time, but this experience demonstrated to me that our *inner* selves are really soft-edged, diaphanous, luminescent energy passengers that are riding around in these (somewhat clunky) human vehicles.

Realizing that unique kind of spiritual *perspective*—looking down on this life—is quite literally the essence of where I want to take you first, so you'll need to get used to using a little of what I'll call "divine imagination" to withdraw sometimes, and assume a position theoretically above and away from your physical situation. That calm, objective outlook won't happen when our head is tightly screwed into the immediate reality that our normal, material reactions demand, so we have to be willing to *detach* (with Love) and move from our hearts out to a saner and safer point of view—free from our urgent impulses, like those inspired by fear or anger. When we practice this, we can instantly engage a completely different form of spiritual "self" in the world of our perceptions, and can be released to live an unfettered life in an easier, much more graceful way.

I'll call this first lesson the lesson of *perspective*.

2) The Lesson of Presence

My second NDE took me to a pretty heavenly place too. Years later, in the midst of a cascading physical reaction brought on by a toxic, self-destructive lifestyle, I found myself once again detaching from my body, only this time I was swallowed up in a brilliant white cloud that was radiantly imbued with reassuring warmth, comfort, and ease. Suddenly, out of the center of the cloud, a kind of screen opened up—definitely a very high state of spiritual technology. Slowly at first, it began to replay forgotten scenes from my life—one after another after another, in a peculiarly *interactive* way.

They were moments that I hadn't wanted to remember, obviously —as I'd forgotten them all until they began playing back again in my ethereal cloud screening room. Rather, they were moments of great *karmic* power—previously insignificant moments where I'd unconsciously made the kinds of choices that had sent me down the difficult road of life I was on at the time. They were passages where I'd created the obstacles to my own potential and growth—and the crazy thing was, they'd all originally transpired in just a couple minutes on some long forgotten day.

Those frozen moments came to life again on that three-dimensional screen, in that strangely celestial place. When I finally awoke (about two hours later), I realized that every single eternal moment is a precious, discrete opportunity for discovery and self-realization. Every instant is a chance to be present for what could be one of the most important lessons our life can present us with, that our larger, eternal Life has to offer us.

I realized that I needed to develop a kind of calm vigilance—to really listen to others and to consciously become a *witness* to my life— so that one of those moments (any moment) doesn't pass unnoticed by the self-absorbed person I can be when I'm on auto-pilot; so that one of those critical Heaven-sent moments doesn't slip by again, unappreciated by a typically clueless, semi-conscious version of myself. I came to understand that every moment can be—and potentially *is*—very, very important.

I call this second lesson the lesson of *presence.*

3) The Lesson of Purpose

My third (and hopefully last) NDE was a harsher and harder experience in every way. The circumstances were painful, and the lesson I received felt like I was being given an unwanted mission—probably because of the place I was at in my life back then, where it seemed like the whole world was against me. At the time, I was living in a place you could almost consider to be a personal hell.

I'd been assaulted by a thug in a public plaza and, after a brief, violent scuffle, was making my escape when I got ambushed from behind and knocked out cold with a blunt object—maybe a tire iron or such—by the rest of the gang, who proceeded to stomp and kick me for the worst part of an hour. Still, with some distant, dislocated sense of the brutality occurring to me, I found myself "on the other side" in a darkish, womblike place—protected and comfortable, but in no way light or cheery. There was a host of benevolent entities encircling me, and although I badly wanted to stay there—to be free of the painful material world I still felt remotely attached to—my hosts would not allow it. They "picked me up" and gently pushed me back into this life with a steady, overpowering force—all the while insisting that *I had not accomplished what I had yet to accomplish.* I sort of "popped through" a membrane back into the world of matter, back onto a concrete sidewalk, with that mission: to become *who I was authentically meant to be.* From that point on, I began to realize that I had to live out my true, divine purpose (no matter how commonplace a life it may seem), primarily for the benefit of others, and to gain my own spiritual freedom.

Each of us has this mission—this blessing, really—to find out how we can best express our life's calling for others, in our own unique and intimately interconnected way. It may not seem special compared to some, but it is what we are all searching for—the real way to bring fulfillment into our life, and into the lives of those we love and care for (in other words, into the life of the world).

I call this third lesson the lesson of *purpose.*

These three lessons of *perspective, presence,* and *purpose,* which I've been fortunate to bring back to you, are meant to serve as the starting point for our explorations into the gorgeous reality that I hope to show you. These lessons are like keystones on the path that can serve to anchor us, locate us, and direct us to a paradise right here in this life, as well as in any life we may move on to. Whenever you're the least bit lost in your travels, any one of these cornerstones can, on its own, put you right back on track—and if you're able to make them all your foundation simultaneously, you'll already be occupying a life that's very close to our goal—I promise you.

Realizing Your Personal Heaven

When we imagine Heaven, these idealized feelings we get may actually be the most *real* part of any new reality we seek; and since feelings are always inspired by something, what things happen in our everyday lives that can give us those sensations of connected bliss? When they aren't simply Love in one of its many forms, they usually come from one of those seldom acknowledged (and seldom appreci-ated) principles at play in our lives—the ones that surprise us and color our day in unexpectedly beautiful ways. They're principles in practice like kindness, humility, honesty, forgiveness, compassion, and service to others, which *are* all Love in its many forms. They're the elements of this beautiful new perspective we plan to create, that we will discover in part I. We'll begin improving our view by opening those doors to Heaven and following our feelings toward a greater sense of well-being.

From there, we will move on to part II and discover the impor-tance of presence as the real means to create the quality of our life. We'll see how our awareness *in this very moment* informs and deter-mines where we've come from in life, where we are, and the amaz-ing potential we can access to empower where we're going. We'll look into the ancient past to discover how presence is the common denominator of all wisdom traditions—the doorway into a timeless state of happiness and fulfillment. Most of our descriptions of what Heaven is, and how we might get there, have been passed down over millennia by countless souls expressing a variety of beliefs, but when we set aside those specifics, almost all spiritual mythologies have a few real essentials in common. Those are the intangibles of an inner variety that don't describe a location, but instead do describe *an expe-rience*. Ancient teachings are often simple mystical formulas, dressed in metaphoric mythology, concealing timeless concepts of personal awareness that are just as contemporary to us now as they have ever been—and will ever be. They're gift-puzzles from the past that we can solve now—ancient clues to a timeless interdimensional reality that's grounded in Love.

While we may have considered that ancient "scriptural" stuff too stodgy and old-fashioned to explore, if we knew how far ahead of our most progressive philosophy much of it is, we might have looked at it from a whole different perspective. The ancient Hindu myth about a warrior and an inner battle of the ages; the supremely scientific intelligence of the Buddha; the deeply relevant mysticism of the enigmatic Gnostics; and the achingly beautiful, heavenly poetry of the world's most popular poet, Jalal ad-Din Muhammad Rumi— these writings aren't really ancient, these archetypal teachers aren't archaic, they're right on point about what's happening *here and now*— in each and every eternal moment.

In part III, with a sense of spiritual perspective, and an appreciation for the power of presence, we'll explore carrying those principles into our everyday personal actions to discover own special purpose. Once we begin to recognize the real magic around us and experience a little bit of Heaven for ourselves, we'll address how we might take up permanent residency there, and spread that heavenly vision to everyone else in our lives. We'll consider what we can do to help our troubled world restore and renew itself to become a little fresher, calmer, and more Heaven-like every day.

When we step back from the planet, it's not so hard to see that we're all part and parcel of very much the same thing here, aren't we? That's the perspective we want to constantly fold into our lives, down here on the ground. Because down here is where it all happens, where it all becomes possible—not only the realization of that Heaven within, but the expression and expansion of our potential Heaven on Earth. And it needn't be a pie-in-the-sky fantasy, not as long as it can be the ultimate attainable human reality for all the life of our planet.

From that solid ground of divine potential, we can witness how our spiritual perspective reaches into everything, from deep within ourselves into the sacredness of all of Life; how compassion and *surrender as a strategy* into the flow of Life's energy will grant us access to a shared intuitive intelligence that can inform not only a more honest appraisal of our past and a more responsibly aware present, but also a heavenly inspired co-creation of our future. On the last leg of our trip, we won't discover the landscape and architecture of Heaven; we'll build it ourselves, and choose to *grow* it—together.

Having been blessed to briefly experience the heavenly nature of Divine Consciousness—particularly witnessing bits and pieces of it within this experience right here—I'm less motivated these days by my experiences of the afterlife than by joyfully realizing the heavenly aspects of Life available to us every day. The afterlife *is* different from life here, but it's the same in this very important way—we are constantly creating the spiritual ground out of which our experience of "reality," and our potential for happiness and fulfillment grows.

This book is about helping you to engage—to help you learn how to make those choices, and to provide you with all the directions I've discovered for reaching that place of joy and fulfillment. It's about finding the doors and pathways—and maybe a few shortcuts—that lead back to the Paradise that we belong to, and making that a possibility that's alive in every moment.

Going to Heaven isn't about going off into a heavenly dream of the afterlife. No, going to Heaven is about being right where you are—wherever that may be—and *waking up*.

PART I:
PERSPECTIVE

The Kingdom of Heaven is already spread out over the whole earth,
but people don't have eyes to see it.
—The Gnostic Gospel of Thomas, logion 113

Once you've been knocked clear out of your body, it can be difficult to get the genie back into the bottle, when the "genie" is your spirit and the "bottle" is your physical self. Looking down on your own lifeless body from a safe, comfortable distance can really change your general outlook on everything. The new perspective presented by this unique experience, and the information it can give you about the true nature of Life, is what we'll explore in this first section. Observing the physical human experience objectively this way allows us to see ourselves and others from a spiritually neutral position. It's all about how to look at life a different way.

For me, it became clear that there are very simple building blocks, classic principles of *being human,* that we can stack up and climb, or ascend like rungs on a ladder, leading up to a transcendent view of everything. We get an infinitely more realistic perspective on the world of this human body we occupy, and who we are in it. The climb is an ascent to a new level of living—the trick is just to keep reaching upward!

– 1 –
Gaining Perspective
Through Simple Principles:
Cultivating a View from on High

The simple truth is that everything we experience and all the ways we react are the product of *what is going on in our minds* at that particular moment. People with disturbed minds live in a disturbed world. People with minds full of love for Life live in a heavenly place already. Most of us occupy a mental space somewhere between those two polarities, and the reason for it is simple but leads to a lot of complications in our lives: It's as if, in a way, *there are two people living inside of our heads.*

No, there aren't!

Yes, there are.

No, there aren't—it's only ME!

In this typical internal dialogue, it's that insistent *me* that can be the source of all the trouble. If we stop and think about it, we can all imagine that at least occasionally there is a crazy person in our heads trying to define who we are, recommending that we do or say all kinds of occasionally inappropriate things. Fortunately, they aren't completely alone in there. There's also a sane, serene, enormously intelligent, and very well-connected person in there too—thank God. This is a form of that famous *duality* that constitutes what's possibly the most precarious and problematic part of human nature, and always has been; in fact, it quite possibly lies at the inspirational heart of our most classic concepts of Heaven and Hell.

What Keeps Us from Going to Heaven?

Simply put, the personal disconnection of our world of material demands from our deep, shared spiritual dimension of light and Love is the cause of every hell we struggle with here on this planet. Aside from experiencing physical pain, there's practically no "hell" that isn't the result of these unconscious human needs—urgent, unfulfilled desires to *get* something, to *be* something, to *protect* something. From the greatest injuries we inflict on the life of our planet to the smallest slights we may perceive as personal affronts or punishments, these desires impair our ability to realize the wonder of our lives. They complicate the greatest challenge we face as human beings: the challenge of *choice*.

It would be almost funny if it weren't for all the terrible things this neediness causes in our lives and in our world, because it really is like the old cartoons where you have a good angel on one shoulder—your caring *voice of reason* who's dependably sane, kind, and helpful—and a little devil on the other shoulder—your *ego-mind*, false self, inner demon (or just call it *will*), fearfully cajoling and criticizing all of the time. You know—that *"me"* that truly can be the crazy person who's taking up way too much space in your head.

But that *me* isn't really *you.*

We all have an essential, positive aspect of our nature that we're heir to, the calm voice of reason that possesses a broad and healthy view of life; and then we have that up-front, anxiously self-enhancing, self-defending part of *me* that we call our *ego*—the voice of fearful instincts that can negatively nitpick at everything we experience, or even covertly sabotage our sense of well-being, and conceal the beauty of Life itself. That range of influence from positive to negative is truly alarming; and while for most of us the negative aspect of our ego is more bothersome than barbaric, any form it takes tends to make us into the kind of person who seldom experiences a "heavenly" moment of peace.

The key to finding our own personal heaven and spreading it into our world comes from rooting out those crazy voices and banishing them, because our ego-minds are insistent mechanisms that will continuously suggest their misguided way is the best way. Without taking some kind of self-corrective actions you may find yourself heading into a constant, semi-conscious state of uncertainty and low-level fear—that is, unless you learn how to *stop listening to your negative ego.*

Many of the problems in our world, most of the things we really could change for the better, are obstacles that we've actually created for ourselves. They're problems that tend to pop up again and again, usually caused by ego demands that drive us toward what we think we need to be happy or "successful," or false challenges that keep us from becoming what we can really be. I'll talk about this throughout the book, but the suggestions in this first section are designed to help you acquire the kind of heavenly perspective that can change your relationship to yourself and the world, and help you stay in conscious contact with the kind and caring angel on your shoulder. It all starts with redefining your view.

What might life's troublesome obstacles look like if they weren't right in front of us, blocking our view and dictating our direction? What if we could turn the volume down on the running commentary that our ego-voice anxiously provides and look at our problems from safely above—like a bird, free and sailing on a divine breeze, surveying all of these distinctly *human* difficulties from a more holistic vantage point? Then, none of those problems would appear to be as insurmountable as they look from down here on the ground, because in truth, they're usually nothing but unnecessary constructions of our minds.

As we are thinking, so we are *becoming,* and the birds and other animals can teach us a lot about that. They find a way within their own conscious perceptions to live in complete accord with nature and the world—to create no damaging complications whatsoever. Perhaps we can take a lesson from them and imagine ourselves more as living simply and appropriately in scale with all the rest of Life— according to our natural needs and attributes.

What if, with no great effort other than employing a few principles and a little imagination, that shift in our point of view could dramatically change practically *everything* about our lives for the better? What if we could adopt a whole new orientation that would simplify and clarify all of our experiences? Is there such a transformational perspective that can change the life we perceive as a series of stubborn challenges into that of a graceful conductor, observing the easy orchestration of all of Life's magical moving parts?

Getting the Best View to Start

In Hinduism, there is a Sanskrit word *sakshi,* which simply means "the witness," and it's a beautifully simple idea, really. It's an idea that you can easily assume as your own, because it's about *who you really are* apart from the demands of your rambling thoughts. Sakshi can suddenly shift your perceptions—your perspective—because it's *the witness* that pays no mind to your moment-to-moment mind. Unlike the incessant ego-voice, it applies no labels or judgments to what it observes. It's just a simple, pure awareness that looks upon all things with an objective compassion and graceful acceptance, as a serene, intuitively analytical eye. It's what I refer to as your "authentic" self, and it's that channel into Divine Consciousness that I believe we're all actually connected by, and are meant to discover and express in this world.

Having had the mixed (but eventually good) fortune of surviving multiple Near Deaths, including my first classic out-of body one, there's a very instructive practice I'd like to pass along that came from being given that chance to look down on my crash site and become "the witness" to my apparently lifeless physical body. When I think about it now, I often engage my imagination to help me become lighter than air again, to liberate my authentic self from the dysfunctional drag of my ego's demands and transcend my material self-centeredness—and you can try it too.

Rising above the Ego: *An Informal Exercise*

Imagine yourself outside of your own body, being your pure, authentic spiritual self, unencumbered by the insistent designs and definitions of your ego-mind. Be as omniscient and objective as you can while observing everything—including yourself. From there, you can look down at the limiting definitions your mind imposes on the vast potential of life spreading out in every direction. You can witness how many possibilities you may be unconsciously surrendering to a narrow set of needless fears and habits. From that point of view—as the objective spiritual entity that you actually are—the world looks much simpler, less threatening. We experience what, in Latin, is called *sub specie aeternitatis*—the actual eternal nature of our authentic self—our channel to an intuitive sixth sense that can be applied as a mitigating filter to the hardships of being human.

When you identify yourself at that level, as a transcendent, authentic self more unified with the Universe than with your physical state of being, the problems and obstacles of life on Earth carry much less power. For example, the guy at work who's always in your face loses the label "antagonist" and is observed as simply demonstrating his need to express the demands of his own experience to whoever will listen to him. It's not just about you, as your ego wants you to think—you just happen to be in his line of fire. Life with this little adjustment will immediately begin to feel much less like it's happening *to you* and much more like it's happening *for you.*

As this imaginary shift in perspective helps free you of the habitual machinations of your mind, you begin to gain a more expansively tolerant consciousness. You acquire an easier acceptance of people—as they are—and of the entire world—as it is. You can be freed from your confining expectations, because your new perspective allows you to witness everyone (including yourself) as part of a greater whole—as fairly inconsequential expressions of a simple human moment, just trying to express themselves. This allows you to isolate and own your particular expression too, and to bring to each moment what you alone can provide to improve things. You no longer have a competitive horse in the race because you're watching the race from spiritual box seats way above the action, with the objectivity of a benevolent, disembodied spirit. You begin to see the entire shape of every problem and all of its tangential contributors, so there's no problem that appears too large or complex to be overcome.

From up there, you can plainly see the unwanted interventions of your ego-mind, as you see yourself below trying to control people you can't control, and situations that are clearly much bigger than you. You witness your ego-mind fearfully judging, comparing, and dictating all kinds of non-essential solutions to non-existent problems. You start asking *Who is that person in my mind and why are they set on complicating things again?* From up there, you might consider dropping something really heavy right on your ego-mind—like all those unnecessary fears your ego wants to weigh you down with all the time. That ought to do the trick.

Free from having a negative, imaginary "reality" whispered in your ear, you needn't worry that you'll lose your passionate direction and become detached from "real life," because this new perspective allows you to see your attachments and passions in a much truer context—alongside everyone else's—and how you may begin to conduct your authentic self, and the elements you really can control, more accordingly.

With the spiritual objectivity of *sakshi,* the nature, the size, and even the origins of your personal obstacles become more apparent, so you can see how they've shaped your past for you, how they can be dealt with better as they pop up now, and how they might be avoided in your future. You become more engaged in your life simultaneously as a whole—past, present, and future. What has worked, what hasn't worked, what you would like to be, and what you probably need to do in order to become that more authentic version of yourself.

Imagining that you're a detached witness up in the sky actually places you on an elevated pedestal, like a conductor above an orchestra. You begin to relate to a "higher self" that empowers your actions, your effectiveness, and your compassionate Consciousness to show up for life with a more direct presence. Any responsibility can be met. Any obstacle can be overcome. Potential setbacks and catastrophes, unimaginable accomplishments, and miraculous joys can be realistically anticipated and gracefully engaged with.

For me, it may be summed up as this resolution: "I resolve to be an open-heartedly objective and compassionate witness of, and entirely engaged participant in, the remarkable, indescribable magic of Life on this beautiful Earth."

The Rewards and Challenges
of Climbing Your Ladder

In my first NDE I found that I was thoroughly *a part of* everything, folded into a limitless shared life so that the boundaries of "me" no longer existed. I felt completely connected to, and completely trusting in, a greater intuitive intelligence—an all-encompassing benevolent *mind* beyond what I had ever experienced in my own small, separate mind. I felt completely liberated, detached from the world of things, which no longer held any interest for me.

I had transcended that duality I spoke of earlier. In that heavenly experience of a graceful dimension existing just above, around, and *within* this one, there was no real matter. There was nothing material about it—and so it was in my experience of Heaven.

From that perspective, material things and situations come into this existence, and pass out of this existence, but only affect me in the ways I think about them and how much I depend on them for my sense of well-being. An extravagant car is a fabulous source of pride until a parking-lot accident turns it into a fabulous repair-shop expense. When we accumulate that stuff of great desire, then we have all that stuff to take care of—and that stuff just keeps coming and going. It becomes the center of our life too easily, instead of what is the real center of all of our lives—the Divine Consciousness I experienced from my bodiless perspective, what we usually all call *Love*.

Wouldn't it be nice, as we struggle to climb above the fray, to just drop that big sack of ego—all those expectations and attachments?

Unfortunately, the fantasy of leaving our tenacious ego-self behind is never so easily realized. We may dedicate our imaginations to ignoring that voice by rising above it, but that can turn into a constant struggle itself, resembling a carnival game of whack-a-mole where every time you smack down a destructive ego suggestion, another one pops up. It can lead to the very thing you're trying to escape—a circular struggle in your own mind, with your ego as a persistent antagonist rather than a positive cheerleader. The conscious recognition of our thoughts as "inner personalities" allows us to become more accustomed to what our antagonistic ego *sounds* like—the negative tone it has (anxious or snarky) and the *content* of what it always wants (self-enhancement or self defense) that lets us catch it and cut it off whenever it starts up again.

Even then it's just a good first step, because constantly suppressing a largely involuntary, deeply imbedded instinct through the pure force of our amazing mental powers—well, that just won't work all the time.

If you want to find Heaven, you're not going to do it by just sitting around and thinking about it—you'll have to take action. You'll have to get up, get out there, and look for actions to take that can boost you upward and help you find a better view of life. Getting to Heaven *is* based on the good deeds you do, so there are actual intuitive ways of thinking and acting that can be considered ladders that we can climb to energize true spiritual perspective.

You might consider the "rungs of the ladder" I'll present in this first part of the book (kindness, humility, honesty, forgiveness, compassion, and service) to be obviously laudable principles, but perhaps a little too soft and fuzzy for handling the hard challenges of the rough 'n' tough material world. Nothing could be further from the truth. These are actually profound, principled actions of enormous power that can transform the harshest and most difficult circumstances of life into experiences of great beauty and miraculous potential. These direct means of ascension can help us to transcend our need for them—to lift us to a place of spiritual perspective where we can kick away the "ladder" and realize our sacred empowerment and dominion. They can actually lead us to the view of a Heaven that we all deserve to inhabit.

These principles—these rungs on our ladder to Heaven, you might say—are all about transforming the obstacles imposed on us by our mindsets and material states into powerful advantages.

We release the conditions imposed on us by anger through kindness, self-centeredness through humility, fear through honesty, remorse through forgiveness, criticism through compassion, and separateness through service.

Removing these obstacles opens up a real view of Life that allows you to see right through material complexities into the *Love*—Rumi's "clear bead at the center"—that actually envelops and energizes everything all the time.

At that point, you become a witness to the material world without being controlled by its ups and downs. You become a witness to the way your desires, your fears—*your thoughts*—can be defining your life in such a limiting way. You realize a new freedom, based on being loved, supported, and connected to the energy of liberated consciousness. All it takes is a little imagination, and a little action.

- 2 -
Kindness:
It's Very Nice to Be Very Kind

I have a good Spanish friend whom I call an old friend because we've known each other for so long, and because, gratefully, we're both getting old. Many years ago when I was a traveling youth, he gave me a gem of wisdom that I've never forgotten. He told me this: "There are two kinds of people in the world: those who will help you when you need help, and those who won't." The truth of that statement has become clearer and truer to me over the years, and if you've ever found yourself in a tough spot in unfamiliar surroundings, you know that the kindness of strangers can make all the difference between feeling safe and secure or lost and abandoned. A helpful stranger can become something of a saving angel to you, and my old friend is just that kind of angel—one of the truly nicest people I've ever met.

For most of us, that's the first thing we associate with any form of "Heaven" as we imagine it—that it would be a really *nice* place, where we would be treated very well and very kindly. Most of the reports of afterlife experiencers, near-death survivors, and the like all have this one thing in common—that in the state of being we call *the afterlife* we felt enfolded into the energy of unconditional Love, acceptance, and kindness. The pervading sense of *kindness* itself is a basic grounding resonance that permeates all good relationships and experiences in any life, here or "beyond."

Where Kindness Comes From

I think most people plan on being nice, and imagine themselves being pretty nice most of the time, but the truth is that we can all get caught up in our own turmoil and forget to actually *be nice,* or conveniently overlook the fact that we may not be behaving well at all. The result is that kindness can seem like a scarce commodity in this chaotic world, so full of all our serious "important" personal transactions.

What any serenity-enhancing practice requires to work is a realistic *conscious awareness* of who we are and how we actually behave—to consciously become aware of how we're really treating other people (and ourselves) in any and every moment. So in order to understand what consciously practicing kindness can actually do for us, let's start by doing something that probably few of us have ever done before. Let's take a good look at what kindness is. If you're like me, you've probably never given much thought to what it actually means to be nice.

Kindness, when we witness it or experience it, probably creates one of the easiest, most understandable, and most accurate impressions that we form spontaneously—often before we even know we're doing it. Think of the times you've happily found yourself saying "They're such *nice* people" and feeling sure that you're right about it. We easily and accurately form such conclusions quickly, based on a first meeting or a passing experience. In fact, wouldn't we all agree that one of life's greatest pleasures comes from meeting really nice people or experiencing moments of real kindness (particularly from a complete stranger)? They're experiences that immediately elevate our lives and instantly inspire a joyful connection—a wave of identification and feeling of *belonging to.*

In a sense then, kindness is the most direct expression we have of unconditional *Love,* especially with people we don't know well. Then kindness serves as an appropriate suggestion of intimacy and acceptance, because an attitude or act of kindness indicates that its bearer is an open-hearted, generous person with a loving and benevolent nature. In fact, kindness is really what we're all hoping to find in one another, in order to experience the ease that comes with being liked and understood. I don't know about you, but I like being liked, and I love being understood.

In the atmosphere of friendly identification and acceptance, maintaining unconditional kindness toward one another is recognition of the hardships we all face as seemingly separate individual passengers on our Earth. It becomes a graceful precondition—an acknowledgment that *this life is not easy*—that we all have our struggles, our good days and our bad days. The atmosphere created by being kind to one another helps us transcend our self-centered view from down here on the ground—where it's easy to feel like the all-consuming center of our own Universe. It instantly elevates us to a point of view where we witness a more complete truth—that we're actually all experiencing pretty much the same problems almost all of the time: keeping a roof overhead and food on the table and finding a little Love and some respect. It's just the names, faces, and places that change.

Kindness itself isn't just a practice or an isolated act, it's a tangible, powerful form of *energy*, rooted in Love—a transformative energy, recognized and appreciated by everyone for how effectively it can improve practically any condition or situation. Everyone naturally knows and acknowledges this power of kindness whether they say so or not, and by applying a little conscious awareness of it, we can see the influence of its energy on every scale, and on every form of life that we participate in.

For example, you can see the power of kindness in a garden (or on a windowsill) where someone with a green thumb lovingly tends to flowers and plants that respond to their gentle care. We constantly witness it (with great anticipation) in the kitchen, as we watch a careful and deliberate cook make something really good to eat, and we experience it in the joy of conspiratorial collaboration when we prepare something delicious to eat together. We selflessly help one another find the tasty joys in life, and happily serve those joys up to one another's delight. That's kindness you can taste.

We witness a very pure form of kindness in the animal world— heartwarming, often unexpected behavior from one animal to another, or from animals toward humans (and vice versa)—that issues from a more direct, inexplicably *divine* source than what we generally contact on our own. There are no ulterior motives in these inter-species interactions, just the energy of kindness profoundly transforming the eternal moment. Elephants, apes, dolphins, lions and tigers and bears (oh my!) demonstrate acts of kind recognition toward one another, across species and even toward humans, every day—they always have and always will.

Human hearts everywhere are constantly being healed by small animals that many people barely consider conscious until they're sad and lonely and are suddenly elevated by the loving energy of a fuzzy cat in their lap or the head of an understanding dog, resting peacefully across their leg.

Showing unconditional kindness to a stranger in need—being the best kind of those "two kinds of people"—connects us to the heart of the Universe, so to speak—the underlying field that is the source of Love in this world and beyond.

Being Nice Is Palpably Powerful!

Kindness is noticeably evident as a palpable energy whenever we enter a room full of strangers—its energy is alive in some rooms, and perceivably not in others. It emanates openly from collections of nice people, while a barren coolness radiates from the looks and body language of people whose hearts need to open up a bit. In the situations that a stand-up comedian might refer to as a "tough room," the conscious application of kindness can create immediate results. Just being sincerely nice to a bunch of sourpusses can disarm their curt defensiveness and shift the energy of an entire meet-and-greet in a noticeably positive direction. Bringing that energy of kindness into tough situations can encourage an almost magical manifestation of more kindness and frivolity—often from the very corners that seem to seethe with distrust or affectation.

An air of identifiable, playful conspiracy arises when you discover the hidden undercurrent of kindness running through all situations—the network of kindly people who have apparently all been in league with one another—whether you were aware of it or not. Love is truly *everywhere* to be found, and kindness is its congenial catalyst.

This makes the energy of kindness perhaps the single most powerfully transformative social and experiential lubricant ever known to humankind (and that may be an understatement). It easily defeats cocktails and weather chat for that title, because those require the energy of kindness to function anyway, as perhaps *everything* does. Ascendant intelligence, empirical expertise, or sparkling wit can't hold a candle to kindness, for without it, they all amount to simply data, or ephemera, or sad self-enhancement of a sort. Even humor, as powerful as we all know it can be, only really works in a transformative way when it's inherently kind. Humor found at someone else's expense or sarcasm posing as humor isn't really funny, it's just agitating—a guilty pleasure whose wrongness makes us laugh (uncomfortably). We're right when we laugh and say "Oh, *that's terrible,*" because that type of humor *is* terrible in a way, and only an application of kindness can righten it and brighten it. Kindness, by its very nature, is never wrong; and when we say "They're killing them with kindness," we're not really talking about the kindness, but about the conditions attached to it.

Lighthearted freedom is the true experience of our spiritual selves, and the moment that kindness creates an atmosphere of loving identification, humor sets in with a twinkle in its eye. Kind people are almost always funny people, and sly glances, well-intended asides, and self-deprecating observations are the language of joyful congeniality alive in heavenly conversation. Life is fun when you're around kind, open-hearted people—especially when you're one of them yourself. The material world is pretty heavy by definition, and kindness lightens the vibrations of any space, allowing humor to sneak in, or stumble in, or just stand there with a little smile and one raised eyebrow.

The energy of kindness makes all the difference in every kind of exploration or interplay, becoming one of the most important factors in our ability to strike out and explore new places and discover new things. Holding a kindly attitude "proactively" out in front of us when we enter into new situations creates a protective, experience-enhancing filter that lets us perceive the positive potential in everyplace we go and in everybody we meet. When we send the energy of kindness out ahead of us into explorations of new places, people, and things, it fundamentally—you could say *alchemically*—rearranges the permeability of personalities, situations, and discoveries of every ilk, even *before* we actually engage with them. In short, our world reflects the kindness that we project into it.

So as a first step in transforming the mundane into the Divine, it's crucial to extend kindness to everyone and *into* everything you experience as a regular practice—like shining a light on everything you see. Send it into every living thing, and even inanimate things you encounter, and watch what happens! Project kind thoughts toward someone approaching you, and see if it doesn't elicit a smile. Respond in a very kind way to someone who wasn't expecting it, and be prepared to suddenly find a new friend. The Buddha was even able to express the power of kindness mathematically when he said: "None of the means employed…has a sixteenth part of the value of loving kindness. Loving kindness, which is freedom of heart, absorbs them all; it glows, it shines, it blazes forth." [4]

I'm not sure just how the Buddha came up with that exact fraction, but I'll go along with it, considering his overall track record. His observations serve as a powerful lesson: Nothing can match kindness for pure transformational power—especially not any method that depends on *force*. Everything material *is energy*; and positive transformation can never come from forcing it—it's a result of caring, cooperative adaptability. But the energy of kindness (the power of Love) generates both forceful strength and compassionate cooperation. In Heaven, *force* is an out-of-work actor, while kindness sets the entire stage.

---

4. Ambedkar, *The Buddha and His Dhamma*, 300.

The Deeper Benefits of Kindness

Often, kindness isn't an attribute that comes easily or naturally to us. There's a wistful understanding that we've all had many opportunities to be *unkind*—and that many of us have exercised those opportunities more than we would care to remember. In fact, with just the smallest dose of self-awareness, our un-kindnesses tend to stand out in our memories in a very uncomfortable way. In our hearts, we recognize that the incapacity for kindness is a crippling spiritual malady, a terminal cause of suffering; and part and parcel of that is the understanding that someone has had to learn—generally the hard way—how to become kind in order to survive and grow spiritually.

For those of us to whom kindness doesn't necessarily come naturally, there is that deep-down challenge we face to learn to become kinder people—we actually have *to earn* that ability through our own suffering sometimes, or to become conscious of the suffering we've caused others. Deep down, we understand the hurt and the damage done, or that can be done, by being unconscious to our own unkindness.

Realistically, the lack of or inability to express kindness is the cause of nearly all the terrible pain, suffering, and needless destruction in our world today. It's an affliction that we can all identify with, one that moves us all away from our possibilities for Heaven.

With grateful optimism in opposition to life's sad inevitabilities, kindly attitudes express those hard lessons we've learned—and the good choices we've made and will likely continue to make. It indicates a kindly vigilance that we apply in our lives in order to create positive change, positive growth; to become better people and to do what we can to make the world a little bit more like Heaven.

You could even call the need to be kind to one another a little self-serving in a way, because practicing it opens us up to unexpected advantages. Kindness moves in a cycle: through us, into the world, into others, and then back to us, where we may unexpectedly realize that being kind to others is *being kind to ourselves.*

The way we look and act in the world is often a projection of our own (sometimes overly harsh) self-judgments. We identify with the biblical maxim "Love your neighbor as thyself" (Luke 10:27), but if we're being tough on our neighbor, it may be because we're really unhappy with ourselves. Likewise, when it's easy to love our neighbor, we need to remember to extend the same consideration *inwardly*, to love ourselves as kindly and automatically as we can love our neighbors.

Being kind to ourselves can become our starting point—our primary means of realizing the benefits of kindness. The moment we give ourselves a break and assume a kinder perspective by consciously overlooking our own harsh self-judgments, kindness begins to cascade. When we become conscious that we've been judging others unfairly, we become open-hearted enough to push our silly self-importance aside, and in that moment we immediately begin to experience the kindness of others. We start to notice all the kindnesses that we'd been overlooking due to our self-centered perspective.

So in a good way, it's a little selfish to be kind to ourselves and to others, because it doesn't only guarantee our own spiritual survival, but the survival of an even greater *Self* that we all belong to. The doors to what we may have thought of as a very exclusive club are open to us—and really have always been open to us, if we'd just had the eyes to see them. Kindness attracts more kindness, and it starts by simply holding those doors open for someone else.

What happens to you when you go someplace where everyone is really nice to one another? At first you may not even believe it's authentic, but when you do, then you just want to go back there again. You may even want to live there—or at least to do your best to make where you live *more like that.* When you try to turn wherever you are into a little piece of Heaven on Earth, kindness is the primary catalyst for that change, within you and around you.

EXERCISE: *Ways of Discovering Real Kindness*

As a means of exercising the power of kindness in your life, I would like to propose that you conduct an experiment over the course of a couple of days. Consciously assume an attitude of unconditional loving kindness toward absolutely everyone you meet—and just watch what happens. Be as nice as possible to everyone you meet—no matter who they are—and see how it can change things for you. Kindly engage with people you may have earlier ignored. Talk positively to the person you're waiting in line with. Pitch in and help someone else whenever you're given the opportunity. In the past I've called this Radical Kindness, and its effects are profoundly transformative—but don't take it from me, try it yourself.

To help you respect the effectiveness of kindness when it comes to positively transforming your life in the working world, try thinking of it this way as an exercise. Imagine that you are about to take a two-day business trip to a conference or seminar, and it's of critical importance that you maintain an attitude of extreme kindness, acceptance, and open-minded teachability toward everyone you meet—in fact, your career, reputation, and material success may depend on it. You've got to make a good impression to be picked for the team and to contribute the skills and qualities that only you possess. Now *be as absolutely kind to everyone you meet*, no matter who they are. Act like everything depends on it, because in a heavenly kind of way, everything does.

Living with kindness toward others in your own heart allows you to feel connected in a way you never have before, and to get a new perspective on the world that some have called "looking at life through rose-colored glasses," by opening up your perceptions. The world won't only be tinted by the color of kindness—you'll also be able to *stop and smell the roses* more often as well, since kindness invites you into an easier, more sensory experience of Life. You'll become the recipient of kindness in return, and occupy a lighter, friendlier, more supportive, more *heavenly* world than you ever knew existed before, even though it's been there all along.

Kindness is the helium of the heart.

– 3 –
Humility:
How a Humble Life
Is So Totally Fabulous

It goes without saying that the moment of a Near Death Experience doesn't stand out as one of your best moments ever. It's certainly not one of life's typical highlights. In situations of life-and-death desperation, considerations of economic class or personal standing disappear. No one is superior to anyone else at the moment they might die, and each of us will face our inevitable and ultimate humbling. Take it from me, that moment of deep humility instantly rearranges your priorities.

Because of the shared etymology of the words *humility* and *humiliation*, it's easy to get their meanings mixed up. The truth is that they describe nearly opposite states of being, despite sharing the same origin. Humiliation, we all know, is a sorry state to be in, and can be a painful place in more ways than one. You could call it a little piece of personal hell—and as far as feelings go, you'd be right about that.

Humility is an entirely different kind of state altogether, less of a physical condition and more of a spiritual presence. It's a centered, grounded emotional attitude whose appearance of quiet calm actually speaks very loudly about an unseen connection of great power and influence, and the potential for fulfillment on a very deep level. Humility, in its truest sense, has the quality of a force of Nature.

When we talk about being humiliated or feeling humiliated, we're talking about our relationship with the world of surfaces. We may feel the shame deeply, but only because our pride is at stake, because we've somehow been competing with ourselves or others in the arena of *ego*, gambling with our self-image in a world of unforgiving comparison. In being humiliated, we feel we've *lost face*, but it was only our "game face" that we lost—a mask that was in some way borrowed by our ego for some kind of competition. When we've altered or concealed our authentic nature in an effort to stand out on a largely meaningless battleground—where standards constantly shift—somebody's got to win and somebody's got to lose.

The quiet person, refusing to play the game, can be wrongly dismissed for "not having what it takes," because what they don't seem to have—attitudes of ambition, aggression, deviousness, and self-centeredness—are actually the very attitudes that create anxiety and unhappiness for both the player and those around them.

On closer observation, the idea that a humble person is somehow weak or ill-prepared for life is a serious misperception, a misreading of the practical strengths of patient awareness and adaptability. The typically negative definition of *surrender* is often wrong-headed too, because it's that *yielding* quality that actually demonstrates the wisdom of surrendering to the dynamic of things as they really are, rather than struggling to control forces that are invisibly beyond us.

Heaven is not subject to the manipulations of our personal design. It's of a far simpler architecture, based on the most solid foundation imaginable: a pragmatic (and mysterious) reality and an honest authenticity. By its nature, being truly humble anchors us to that essential ground of being, rather than setting us adrift in a precarious kind of purgatory, on an ever-shifting surface subject to forces that may suddenly overturn and swallow us and our pride or sweep away the fragile structures that we believe will protect or enhance us. "Puff yourself with honor and pride and no one can save you from a fall," said Lao Tzu, the wise old man of Taoism.[5]

---

5. Lao Tzu, *Tao Te Ching*, verse 9.

The Changing View of Humility

At different times in our journey, I'll refer to *fields* in kind of a quasi-scientific way, as in the quantum field or the field of gravity. I believe that humility is a similar type of natural phenomenon—a grounding field of interaction with our most authentic nature. As a medium for the creation and support of our life, it defines success in a whole different way. Humility allows us to live in a parallel dimension that's more secure and sensible than the transient, threatening material world; and, as you may have gathered, I don't believe that Heaven is a place, but instead is *a dimension of being* that seems apart from, yet actually is, the living Source of "this mortal coil" we inhabit.

Humility, when it's understood to be this grounding medium, can become the source of our personal authenticity. It provides a clearer understanding of who you really are, and the best conditions for becoming who you want to be. It enables and inspires a level of deep wisdom—an *intuitive intelligence*—for all the choices you make.

Stop and think for a minute about your favorite people, and not necessarily in the sense of who's fun at a party or who seems to have what it takes to "score" in the areas of romance or finance. Don't get me wrong—people who are entertaining or beautiful or materially successful are great to be around, and fun to actually *be* sometimes, but if you've ever touched on that yourself you know those winning attributes are actually surface conditions that come and go, and that the appearances of your outsides are sometimes just an effort to conceal or ameliorate the true condition of your insides. Seeking attention can look like desperate self-promotion, and the feelings of superiority it brings are usually too momentary and elusive to garner any real sense of fulfillment or lasting happiness.

I'm talking about those people who may not appear to have what it takes on the surface, but instead have *a certain something*—a quality and ease of being that you deeply admire and respect. They have a difficult-to-define quality that you can't help but find profoundly attractive. It's not a tenuous fantasy of success or gratification, but a sense of buoyancy—a steadiness, and a powerful alignment with the world as it is that allows them to define the world *they want to live in themselves.* They seem to possess an almost elemental (or *eternal)* charisma—like they're members of a secret club, or woven into a comfortable, invisible fabric of Life that the rest of us don't know about. They're not without fears and deep concerns, like everybody else, but they don't seem to worry about it so much. They seem to know they're being carried in a benevolent flow. They have endless access to an easy, reliable power. They have *faith.*

That calm, dependable faith speaks volumes for the power of humility, and on top of being extraordinarily attractive, it's very persuasive, spontaneously generous, intuitively creative, and effortlessly influential—all pretty heavenly attributes, I'd say.

You may not hear a lot about these people, even when they influence your life and the lives of many others for the better. We tend to conflate being well-known with being successful, but that's only true in terms of our fickle, hard-sell material world. In the idyllic dimension that contains and spreads beyond this world (which we may call the Field of Love and Consciousness), those very humbly successful individuals speak softly but carry no shtick. They're connected to everyone else by character traits such as compassion, acceptance, humane engagement, justice, and, of course, kindness. They are "right-sized" in the world, and as such are in sync with an unimaginably greater dimension that constitutes the matrix of a loving reality.

When you think of the times you've spent with the humble people in your life, there are only good memories to be found. That's because of the attitude of loving kindness they always show you and everyone else—an attitude you may suspect they've earned *the hard way.* When people are forced to painfully confront their own shortcomings and imperfections, it gives them the perspective to witness the imperfections of others with complete tolerance and acceptance—with an affectionate understanding, as though they can completely identify with anybody's problems, because they can. Truly humble people understand the challenges we all face in this life, and are always willing to listen and help if possible. They know this life ain't easy for anybody.

When we think of those people (which we should do more often) and try to be more like them, we're aligning ourselves with the citizenry of Heaven. Just stopping and considering the energy of humility they radiate can suddenly defuse the chaotic quality of the material world. Consciously generating it yourself can profoundly change your life and the lives of those around you—just as yours is changed by being around them.

While it's easy to admire someone who effortlessly demonstrates real humility or someone who lives a humble but accomplished life, it's a lot trickier to become authentically humble in our own lives. How can most of us—struggling along as we do—find real humility in ourselves?

How to Find Humility

For me, finding humility is a lot easier when I become aware that I'm not being very humble. For example, if I tell you that I'm on a sincere search to find deep humility within myself, I know that's not being humble. In fact, (in my case) when I start a sentence with "I," chances are I'm going in the wrong direction already. The best way to start finding humility is by simply shutting up and listening—*really* listening—to other people, and then, when it's my turn to speak, to be consciously aware of whether what I'm about to say is a contribution or is just another means to enhance myself in some subtle (or unfortunately explicit) way. Then I can choose whether I really need to say it, or better yet, not to say it at all.

This doesn't mean that you never share your projects or concerns with anyone, just that you don't do it in a way that's promoting a kind of one-upmanship. Here's an important tip to consider while you're trying to find Heaven in the playing fields of the material world: *there is no competition in Heaven.* As with all bad habits, you must become consciously aware that you're doing it—that you're choosing some form of self-promotion again, which really looks more like desperation. Here's another important no-brainer: *there is no desperation in Heaven.*

Even with self-awareness it's a difficult issue to master—becoming humble and merging into the field of humility—because it isn't a function of intellect. Instead it's a feeling, a power, a state of being that has to arise from within.

Most of us (like me again) discover our authentic humility by accident, in not-so-graceful ways that eventually point us toward grace. It often takes the form of an experience that's so contradictory to the search for happiness that we avoid it or try to move past it with such haste that we overlook its true potential. It's the opportunity we get when unavoidably awful things happen to us, when we justifiably feel like life really hurts. It's when things really go wrong, or should I say, it's the silver lining to when things really go wrong.

This is a miraculous and beautiful world we get to inhabit, without a doubt, but it's also fraught with terrible passages and what appear to be injustices of the worst kind all around (including the final and "worst" injustice of all—death). Unfortunately, none of us gets to escape these experiences. Perhaps all the bad stuff isn't just pointless pain and misfortune, but instead is a kind of gateway to the realization of our authentic nature—an opportunity to discover our suppressed power and potential. After all, from the perspective of being a human being, wonderful feelings and terrible feelings are always coming and going in a fairly predictable way. It's not a big surprise when things turn tough; in fact, I can be more surprised when things go really well—even though I know good and bad things occur with the same natural frequency.

It is a sensory world, and these alternating polarities-of-being naturally open and close on all our important lessons and opportunities. But notice how we don't tend to learn much about handling life's ups and downs when things are going really well. It's as though we need to be thrown against the rocks of fate once in a while for it to register. Then, and often only then, we get "broken open" to experience true humility—like it or not.

When awful things happen to us—when we're unexpectedly laid off from a "secure" job, when we lose a loved one in an unfair way, when we're suddenly victimized by bad health, when we "fail" financially or are heartbroken by a relationship that's on the rocks, or if we just feel forced to confront what (at the moment) seems to be our "failed" life—it's at those times that the pieces of a life that seemed to fit together so well lie scattered across the landscape of your immediate future. Who you are "supposed to be," what you do, who loves you, who supports you, the style in which you live—your concepts of how you fit into the world suddenly don't seem to make sense anymore.

Unavoidable powerlessness in the face of cruel Fate evokes a deep, personal response in everyone who's ever lived through it, where unexpectedly, involuntarily, you're forced to discover real humility at its most profound level. The state of deep humility is thrust upon you when you don't have any alternatives left. There's nothing you can do but face the music, standing as firmly as you can on the ground of your most basic being—with all pretense of specialness or entitlement stripped away. It's just *you* now, facing life on Life's terms.

At that moment, there's nothing left to block your view, so *look around* and appreciate the view—that's the field of true humility you're standing in, at last.

Although it sure may not seem like it, experiencing that state of absolute humility is a great gift, a state of grace in which there's no longer any external importance attached, no pretense of "winning" (even though you may be a bigger winner in every way because you're suddenly *free*). You are reduced to the simplest condition of egoless selfhood; and that's when you attain a perspective that only humility can give you—a realization of the simplest, most fundamental principles that energize your personal survival and happiness at their deepest level.

You are forced to confront a powerful, more appropriate respect for all life; an unconditional identification with everyone else who's ever been in the same difficult spot; a real understanding of the importance of Love; and a resolve to meet the challenge of surviving the moment with an honesty, openness, and willingness you couldn't have imagined before your "fall." It's the gift of an involuntary faith that you can only find by becoming profoundly vulnerable. You have no choice except to *authentically be who you really are.* Almost immediately the game and its unnecessary rules are forgotten, because they weren't what you needed in your life anyway. Who wins, who loses...who cares?

Then comes your chance to recognize the power and potential of true humility, to embrace it, and, like the mythical phoenix rising, to use it to build a world for yourself based on what you've learned, on who you really are and who you want to be. In the aftermath you inevitably find a better world for you, and for everyone else around you.

Working with Humility

Zen Buddhism uses the metaphoric image of a pond whose surface reflects our lives—our actions and reactions, our thoughts, and our fears. When the surface is choppy with the fragmented reflections of our chaotic world, humility calms the waters from the bottom up, as we sense the calm, secure stillness that lies beneath it all. The "bottom" is always there, and has always been, and really isn't such a bad place to inhabit after all. It's very serene there, and you can just *be yourself.* Contentedly occupying what we once thought was a hard place and consciously choosing to reject the troubled, imaginary surfaces of things bestows a real grace upon us. We recognize that *Love* is the true medium of life that flows underneath, around, within, and through everything. Then the surface of our pond smoothes out as we become a channel of that humble power.

"On the highest throne in the world, we still sit only on our own bottom," said Michel de Montaigne.[6] From that "bottom"—whatever form it may take—we can truly celebrate this delicate condition we all share, and cycle back to where all Love lost will be rediscovered

---

6. Montaigne, *Essais*, book 3, chapter 13.

tenfold. These humbling experiences allow us to accept our own frailties and imperfections so that we can easily and joyfully accept them in others.

Once we're able to release ourselves and others from the false expectations foisted on us by material life, we may even become one of those people we've always admired, the kind of people we may hang around with in Heaven—not necessarily rich or successful in a material sense, but possessing an understanding of Life's real values.

The most angelic man I ever knew was a tall, elegant, extremely warmhearted fellow named Phil who was very well known and very much loved in downtown Manhattan. After his passing, about five hundred people assembled at his memorial service in the Great Hall at Cooper Union, where Abraham Lincoln once spoke. There were wonderful singers, a chorus, speakers, and funny stories, and a little film was shown about how Phil had been lifted out of a life of alcoholic misery to become the primary creator of a program that saved thousands of "lost" men's lives.

Phil had lived quietly and simply, personally mentoring dozens if not hundreds of men and women over nearly fifty years of unselfish service, receiving little or no compensation for most of it, but merely passing along the gifts of a grateful life that he felt had been granted to him. He received very little public acknowledgment from anyone who didn't know what he'd been up to all those years, but when he died, the *New York Times* wrote the longest obituary I've ever seen for a person I actually knew.

Phil's demeanor was always that of loving kindness, with an attitude of a cautious but easy vigilance against the pitfalls of pride and self-centeredness. Like anyone who exhibits enough humility, Phil had a deep understanding of life that grew from rocky ground and didn't flourish fully until later in his life. It can happen like that—humility finally catches up to us in our busy lives, and as our life's direction naturally moves away from ambition and toward meaning, it shakes us awake, liberating us from the bondage of self-centeredness.

At the service there was a funny story told that illustrated Phil's authentic warmth and wisdom as well as his playful spirit:

When a brash, flamboyant protégé of his impatiently stormed up to him and proclaimed, "I'm tired of being so damn *good!*" Phil smiled and quietly said, "Me too."

We don't have to look far in the world of power and politics to see the profound effects of humility. We have Mahatma Gandhi, Nelson Mandela, Mother Teresa, and many other powerhouse examples of self-surrender and spiritual ascension—and not a braggart in the lot. We can find real humility in spiritual leaders closer to home, like in our favorite priest, rabbi, imam, monk, or swami. We see it in our quiet but effective community leaders, and we see it in the simple, loving generosity shown from neighbor to neighbor every day, in every neighborhood in this world (and beyond).

Who would have ever thought that a humble little character trait like *humility* could lead to true happiness, and that it could actually activate a "sixth sense," enabling our experience of an entirely new dimension of an easy, infinitely more fulfilling life, where suddenly it becomes possible for us to become *who we authentically are*. In that dimension we're no longer separate, searching individuals, but instead loving, giving, creative, contributing pieces of a Divine Wholeness. In that dimension of Life, we're all simply expressions of a single Love-based reality. And when you find the gift of humility, you'll become a citizen of Heaven too.

EXERCISE: *Ways of Celebrating Real Humility*

There are a couple easy, straightforward exercises that can help you gain an awareness of humility and engender more of it in yourself, and one is to begin by simply consciously identifying and objectifying it. Think of the people who've had the greatest lasting positive influence in your life, and objectively assess their level of humility. When you watch media, notice the energy of different "important" people, and notice if your intuition prompts you away from those who (subtly or not so subtly) suggest their own importance and toward those who calmly radiate deeper qualities of wisdom and compassion.

As a personal practice, for a day or two try to consciously avoid beginning any sentence with "I." Remain as vigilant as possible for as long as you can, and notice how the focus of your life shifts from your own anxieties to a healthier regard for the well-being of others. Watch your sense of camaraderie become easier, as more friendships, opportunities, and a feeling of calm connectedness take hold in your day-to-day life. People will come to rely on you more, and seek your company and advice—and you'll find joy in playing that role for them.

– 4 –
Honesty:
The Gift of Honesty
Is Really No Lie

Have you ever been caught in a lie? *Oops.* If you have—and I'm assuming we all have (hopefully not too recently or regularly)—then you know that it's really quite impossible to "be in Heaven" at those times. That simple truth could be the end of this chapter, I suppose. I've been tempted over the years to add to the stories of my NDEs, and sometimes I've found myself unconsciously embellishing—but each time I have to catch myself and stop. When reporting on the eternal, honesty is a sacred trust.

On one occasion long ago (in an entirely different life I was living), I got myself caught in a whopper. I had dropped into a very nice gathering with a group of accomplished, well-appointed, well-spoken people who were friends of some friends. For some unknown reason I began pontificating authoritatively on a subject I knew practically nothing about, and once I got going, I felt compelled by sheer bluster to dig myself into a very deep hole. It was about financial matters that I was completely unqualified to discuss, as I found myself offering opinions on some monetary funds that I actually knew nothing about. Not a good start.

As we may know, braggarts and bullies are simply expressing their own fears about their lack of accomplishments, or effectiveness, or ability to control things the way they want, and in this case I was guilty on all charges. At one point, as I was discussing the qualities of an investment fund that I pretended to know about, a well-appointed young man across the table politely suggested that I didn't know what I was talking about *because he was actually the manager of that fund.* All eyes knowingly turned to me as I experienced a moment of utter humiliation—without any humility at all.

I didn't get up and leave immediately, although it would have been welcomed, I'm sure. For some reason I felt the need to hold my ground, as though I had somehow been right, which I plainly wasn't. Some mechanism of self—my ego—wanted to hang on to my fabrications like there'd been something justifiable about them, like I'd somehow been helping everybody. The moment I recovered my wits enough to see through that minor hell of self-deception, I was dropped into actual humility and instantly became teachable. In that very moment I grew (up) into a person who would make a sincere effort to avoid such foolish lies, if at all possible, from that point on.

How (and Why) to Never Tell a Lie

We all know the direct, practical benefits of practicing honesty as a life strategy—mainly that we avoid difficult and embarrassing situations like the one I've just described. It naturally makes life a lot easier—telling *the truth*—because we cleanly avoid the complications that come along with stretching it until it breaks. We all know how exhausting it can be, first to inflate a lie to the point that it becomes airborne, and then to keep it aloft in every direction we sent it; especially when we know that at any moment—usually the worst one possible—it's bound to burst and leave us with that silly look on our face again.

In fact, holding to the ideal of constant honesty gives us a perspective that turns lying into a tough job. It activates our own BS detector, because when we're consistently honest, our own powers of discernment tune themselves to a higher, more accurate wavelength. The lies of others (and particularly our own) become painfully obvious and practically blow up in the room.

Carrying that perspective forth onto the path we travel not only keeps our road smooth in the present but lets us *project* a clearer path with fewer pitfalls and calamities into the future. Being honest allows us to consciously co-create what lies ahead of us, instead of dragging along the lies we thought we'd left behind. Expanding on that geographic metaphor for honesty's effects lets us witness the urge to fabricate our own specialness as a mistaken desire to "gain the higher ground"—one that actually forces us to negotiate a more difficult landscape, filled with detours and dead-ends. Simple truthfulness lays out a smooth, direct road toward our goal.

In truth, honesty is the heart of directness and effectiveness as well as kindness and respectfulness, because most people will happily help advance a truthful cause, and because almost everyone can spot a liar a mile off—and naturally no one appreciates the inherent insult in being manipulated. This is stuff that everyone learns *the hard way*.

If you recall, in my second Near Death Experience I was given a kind of interactive picture show of certain parts of my life, and not the greatest hits but instead occasions when I was not honestly present in my reality. What that means to me is that in some mysteriously effective way all our actions are kept track of. Whether or not they're entered into a quantum data matrix (aka *Akasha*, the Akashic records, the big book of our lives), there does exist an accounting of our karma. That was the source of my "life review." It is a track record of sorts, the results of the causes and effects of our life choices. The seeds we plant determine how we grow toward our potential. Before you can realize Heaven, you have to accept that accounting, and really take it to heart.

No one in Heaven breaks a promise or makes promises they know they can't keep. No one omits or fabricates parts of the truth to materially benefit themselves or to serve *who they think they are*. No one consciously makes a choice to mislead another "for their own good" or "because they deserve it." Benjamin Franklin may have been right when he said *Honesty is the best policy*, and it is a kind of eternal life policy that continuously pays off.

No one is perfect, not even the people you'll find in Heaven, but they always try their best to be honest with others, and especially with themselves. They recognize our tendency to live in a state of self-protective *denial*, and consciously free themselves from that urge. If they should ever find they've succumbed to it, they turn to their willingness to find out *why*. The pain of denial comes from accepting our own ignorance as the truth through sheer force of our will, while getting honest with ourselves sets us free. Our willingness overcomes our willfulness.

When I summed up the lessons from my embarrassing dinner party, I still suggested the possibility that there may be lies that can't be avoided—lesser lies, more acceptable lies, smaller lies that could somehow be justified, even necessary little lies of a benevolent nature. You know, lying to you "for your own good." But playing with degrees of deception is a shady, slippery slope. Not coincidentally, the person who most wants to profit from my "justified" lies almost always turns out to be the manipulative part of *me*.

It turns out that many of us have a natural-born liar living right inside of us.

How I Can Get Honest with Myself

Ego is from the Latin word simply meaning "I," and according to Freud our ego is supposed to mediate between how and why we want to gratify ourselves and how and why we ought to know better. The source of the real truth is much greater than anything our little brains can create, and I call that greater, innate knowledge we all share "intuitive intelligence" as a collective resource or "conscious awareness" as a personal practice. I think of my *ego-mind* as the prevalent voice in my head that wants to be my authoritative interpreter of the outside world—as it wants me to see it. In that case, I can often depend on him to be just *the crazy guy in my head*.

I talk about him (my ego-mind) kindly in the third person because I know that he isn't really *me*, but instead can be the instigator of a reality that's sometimes accurate but often fearfully delusional. If he existed as a person outside of my head, I might recognize him as an anxious sort, prone to jumping to conclusions. Presumably, he acts with my best interests in mind, but many times when I trusted him to be the source of my best thinking I ended up making very bad choices. Later, I realized that I actually knew better all along thanks to my *intuitive intelligence,* or that I would've known better had I exercised some *conscious awareness.*

Problems arise when we think our ego-voice *is who we really are,* when it's actually the expression of instinctive habits we accumulate in our lives. The way our ego functions at a subtle or subconscious level can be particularly troublesome when we realize that we've been fabricating stuff to suit our fantasies—realities that are being pointed out when our conscience is bothering us. An unrestrained, unexamined ego will authoritatively tell you *what other people think of you* and what they are thinking *about* you—without knowing the truth at all. The truth is that most people are far too busy worrying about themselves (as we all normally tend to be), and you're not even on their radar. Honestly, very little in our lives is as important or in need of correction as our egos might want us to believe. In a more heavenly setting, everyone can see right through the ego, and when every life is illuminated by the clear light of truth, *everyone is important.*

While I don't pretend to know the actual internal mechanisms of how or why we lie to others and to ourselves, what I am attempting to suggest is less along the lines of clinical psychology and more along the lines of maintaining a sound *spiritual condition* as the simple solution to these mental complexities. Spiritual principles like humility and honesty give us perspective on our subtly complicated deceptions.

Self-Examination Inspires Honesty, and Vice Versa

Trained psychologists study and categorize human behavior to great benefit, and neuroscience is rapidly mapping the human brain with the aid of technology, but what about the intricacies of the human heart? What of our deepest motivations? After all, you can unpack somebody else's bags, but you'll never know where to put everything away. Only *you* can know and change those things about yourself—and that's the case with most forms of unconscious self-enhancement and self-protection, commonly perpetrated by self-deception. The truth is that *you* know *why you're telling that lie*—and if you become willing to pursue it down that twisting rabbit hole to the source of your fears, you can expose and neutralize those dishonest impulses. Otherwise, your delusional ego will keep you separate from the truth, and may take you for a long, punishing ride in the wrong direction.

Sometimes your ego may misdirect you to behave in a manner contrary to common sense, ignoring the lessons of your past and acting out on some damaging impulse almost automatically, acting habitually from old beliefs that aren't even based in fact. At a deep level *you know* that you're acting irrationally, but you feel like you "have to do it," because your misdirected ego keeps proffering the action as some kind of solution to an imaginary threat or as a form of relief for an unbearable situation. Then, those fears can take command and separate you from the air and the light that simple honesty can reliably provide when you become willing to really look at the situation.

Allow me to use myself and the self-deception that created my embarrassing dinner party as an example. I grew up in a situation where it seemed no one really showed a great deal of interest in whether I did well at anything. It felt like other kids got lots of guidance and encouragement, while I felt like I experienced a general attitude of disinterest and mild disapproval. That's not very comfortable to admit, but it does point to the source of the painful dinner-party lies I told. I think I lied at that dinner party because I grew up accustomed to concealing uncomfortable truths about where I came from, and the low self-esteem that grew out of that led me to desire acknowledgement—even at the risk of my pride. My ego left me little choice but to scramble and inflate my sense of self. Now I'm comfortable with it all, because being honest with myself (becoming conscious) about the source of the impulse to "protect and enhance" has liberated me from letting that rough edge of childhood define the rest of my life. It sounds simple enough when I explain it that way, but it wasn't. It actually took years for me to see that truth.

I needed to chase that impulse down, because letting those life-defining truths continue to pop up in painful ways (when I least expected them) disqualified me from experiencing a heavenly life—even though they may not have been "my fault." They were—and are—nonetheless, my *karma*. They're the result of the causes and effects in my life that I must bring into conscious awareness in order to redirect my actions appropriately. If I don't, they can remain as fearful self-delusions that I refuse to recognize and that continue to strengthen and repeat with predictably painful results.

You see, they're wrong about one thing (whoever *they* are): denial *is a river*—a river that can carry you through cycles of troubled, inauthentic life separated by your own ego from the Love that all of us deserve to reveal and rejoin. If you ignore the causes you create (say people are always asking you to try to be punctual), you'll continue to miss the part of the lesson where you learn what it means to really respect others.

When we become willing, we can dive down into those depths with conscious awareness and swim around those old formative experiences and check them out. If we're being really honest with ourselves, we only need to hold our hearts open and allow the truths our ego conceals from us to reveal themselves. Then we can embrace them, let them go, and swim back up into the light. From that point on, as we remain willing to look honestly at how our past may be coloring our present, we can stand tall on top of the same past that used to drag us under, and learn how to use that unsteady surface as a foundation for building an honest, authentic life.

EXERCISE: *Ways of Uncovering Real Honesty*

As a remarkable insight-building exercise for developing honesty, focus before you speak, and be consciously aware of what you're about to say. Restrain the urge to say it for a second or two, and put it to a kind of quick test: Is it rigorously *true?* (I actually know very little about stock funds.) Is your version of the truth partly augmented or partly omitted? Did you really see that performer two times, not three? Did you actually *finish* that book? Are you turning the truth a little to one side or the other, to reflect yourself from a better angle? When you're really honest with yourself, you may be surprised at how many little white lies (or even whoppers) unconsciously crop up in everyday conversations—and how much lighter you'll feel when you consciously edit them out of your story.

Another exercise is to consciously examine your motives to determine whether your intuitive intelligence is at work or your ego is altering reality for your own self-defense or self-enhancement. For example, when you have a strong first impression or a gut reaction to a person or a situation, keep it in mind and then objectively note whether your impression was accurate or not. How accurate you are informs your awareness about what honest intuition "sounds like," and when ego is subtly, selfishly manipulating the truth. Become more willing to consider difficult questions about yourself and others, such as *Is this person acting inappropriately, or is it really me who's at fault? Could it be my own fragile ego, deviously "defending" me? Could I be agreeing to something that I don't really believe in, or that I don't know much about, just to make a good impression on someone else?* Exercise spiritual perspective when you objectively look at the results of your interactions—if you have to justify your motives, it's probably your unhealthy ego talking.

These exercises help you to have faith in your intuitively healthy ego, your "still, small voice" when it may tell you *This is not the right time for me to tell this person this painful truth. It will come out in a better way at a better time.*

– 5 –

Forgiveness:

It's For Giving … and For Getting

By practicing kindness, humility, and honesty, you begin to get pretty close to a heavenly experience, but there are still a couple of tricky forks in the road that can misdirect you from Paradise. Developing a more heavenly nature means understanding that everyone takes a wrong turn now and then (usually without even knowing it) and that we needn't be too hard on ourselves or others. No one is perfect—not even in Heaven. Real candidates for serenity never entertain the notion of perfection, but instead wholeheartedly identify with the *imperfections* of our human form and the challenges that life poses for everyone seeking the way. They are all for giving the right directions by happily *forgiving* the wrong ones.

When we move through life unconscious of our slips into selfishness and of the lies (large and small) we may have been telling ourselves and others, we may cause a few injuries along the way and have had injuries inflicted upon us by other wayward travelers. When that happens, as it will, we can latch on to an injury with a possessiveness that sends us off course for a week, a month, or, in some particularly tragic cases, an entire lifetime (or, when it comes to reincarnation, *many* lifetimes). Our potential for happiness is taken hostage by an injury—real or imagined—rather than released into the lighter-than-air freedom that is the hallmark of a heavenly existence. Victimhood is always the wrong path to take, and we need to recognize it when it's defining our direction. We have to consciously choose the high road instead, but it's not always an easy thing to do.

In many cases we're entirely justified to feel hurt and form resentments about what someone did to us or how unfair life can be. It seems unlikely (or unjust) that we'd forgive all the small but personally "critical" injuries inflicted on us—much less the truly unforgivable atrocities that the human race can, and does, mete out upon all of Creation. Regardless of how justified our sense of outrage over an injustice or injury may be, we can never find a path into serenity by traveling in the direction of pain—we'll just find more pain there, and continue to propagate it, living with that "dis-ease."

You Already Know
How to Forgive and Be Forgiven

In the case of many of life's most vexing problems, a different perspective could reveal answers we might have already, so it shouldn't be a surprise that a good way to find forgiveness is to look for it among your own personal experiences. Spiritual solutions are usually right in front of you; they're just a little hard to recognize sometimes. As for forgiveness, at one time or another everyone of us has been compelled to seek it for ourselves, especially when we've needed it to move forward—when we realized that we couldn't go on without it.

Recall a time when you committed a wrong—how you wished you could take it back, but you couldn't, and your only option was to ask for forgiveness so that you could be released from the wrong you committed, to move your life forward in the right direction. When you remember that feeling of being forgiven, *reach back* into the release you felt in your heart, and from there you'll intuitively know how to release an injury or injustice that's been done to you. *You know what it feels like to be forgiven and thus how to forgive.*

An injury may never go away completely. Sometimes we don't want to completely forgive and forget a real injustice—that would be denying the lessons we learn the hard way. But we mustn't let it follow us around in our search for happiness and continually push us in a dark direction. We mustn't be held hostage by resentments when we can be free to continue much more lighthearted pursuits!

Transcendence is what's really at work behind the scenes when we're talking about the offering of forgiveness. Like the *sakshi* (witness) I spoke of earlier, forgiving is a consciously aware spiritual action taken by our higher self for the benefit of our lower self that also helps other people's lower selves find their higher selves. It's an action that redirects *both* the giver and the receiver by giving each one the ability to realize the wrong direction they may have gone in *by lifting them both up* to a spiritual perspective that allows them to see a superior path. Naturally, that lift may come for the giver and receiver at different times. The *one doing the forgiving* gets a boost first, because they're instantly released from being defined by pain; then later, the *one who's being forgiven* realizes that they're free too—that they've been released through a spiritual act of identification and compassion.

It takes a little time, sometimes, until one day we realize that, surprisingly, we've *spontaneously forgiven* an injury that had been holding us back—without ever having given much thought to it. Just like that we find that we're free to travel on, no longer encumbered by our past, but in a way *energized* by the realization that the injury has simply passed on.

That isn't just fuel for your trip to Heaven, it's proof of our essentially transcendent spiritual nature—real evidence that if we follow a few simple and organically occurring principles, we'll naturally proceed on an upward trajectory to meet our most authentic state of being. These "aha!" moments open our eyes to see that we've always been on our way to Heaven; in fact, *we may even be in Heaven already* in a way—we just haven't been able to realize it until *now*.

"To forgive is to set a prisoner free and discover that the prisoner was you," says Lewis B. Smedes,[7] and in this doubly effective way

---

7. Smedes, "Forgiveness: The Power to Change the Past."

forgiveness is both for *giving* the proper directions to a fellow traveler who's temporarily lost and for *getting* a better view of the road ahead. From this greater perspective we can see that getting stuck with the bill, or not getting that raise, or being dumped by a significant other are all situations that occur everywhere on such a small scale that they can scarcely be seen from Heaven, and may well be the very thing that allows you to find your own divine path and purpose.

An Answer to Painful Resentments

While it's easy to draw convenient traveling metaphors for these hard-fought battles for forgiveness—for giving it or getting it—the real challenge comes from living through the discomfort of it all. That's because the pain caused by a wrong inflicted is not just theoretical, it's real. It's a deep-seated anxiety that volcanically bubbles up and interferes with even the simplest duties—and pleasures—of Life. That agitation complicates everything, and will continue to do so until you release it (forgive) or relieve it (ask for forgiveness). Consciously imagining a transcendent spiritual perspective may be the best way to *de*activate that anxiety, since every other effort may be too darn close to that ever-churning ground. The Buddhist ideal is simple: *detach with Love*. Rise above it, and naturally do it as soon as possible.

What's a fast, effective way to deal with pain when you're crawling through the battleground of real hurt and anger and disappointment? Well, the best strategy may come from the tough trenches of the drug and alcohol recovery community in the counterintuitive form of a "fox-hole prayer"—that is, to *pray for your perpetrator*. That's right (as crazy as it may sound), whether what you're suffering from is as small as the droppings your neighbor's dog leaves on your lawn or as large as the bombs being dropped on innocent civilians, the most direct route to a realization of a divine release is to take the action of *praying for the source of the pain*. Pray for forgiveness for those who injure others.

It doesn't matter what your denomination is, or whether you even have one; it's the actual *act* of praying for the offender, the dictator, or even the disease that's doing the damage that can do the trick. The *action* of saying a prayer for them to find their own divine direction activates a form of spiritual transcendence that releases you from the pain of your expectations and demands—your wish to control the uncontrollable.

In Heaven, the angels (who were once where we are now) are constantly praying for the souls of those who are doing wrong and assisting those who are trying to do right—not always in visible ways, but they are always right there, hearing your prayers over your shoulder, so to speak. There's a direct avenue between here and Heaven, a divine crossroads where turning toward forgiveness will work to relieve your pain (and everyone else's) in both the long and the short run.

The First Person to Forgive Is Yourself

There is a toxicity in this world that's caused by pride, anger, greed, gluttony, lust, envy, and sloth (to put it in seven familiar terms), all of which are conditions that everyone suffers from to some degree at some time, and all of which require generous applications of forgiveness. There is also a solution that begins with your looking *within* for forgiveness—that is, *forgive yourself first*, then *forgive everyone else*, too.

No one escapes the pain of having done wrong, but there is a chemical reaction, an *alchemical shift*, you might say, created by finding both sides of that two-sided injury within yourself. If you can turn that identification into compassion, and then turn that compassion back toward yourself, a dark cloud you may have felt yourself living under will break open, revealing a luminous sense of possibility. You reduce your personal toxicity through self-forgiveness, and instead of being an unwilling participant in pain, you become a walking, talking antidote for it. This relationship between your transcendent spiritual self and your everyday personality is wonderfully expressed by White Eagle in his book *The Quiet Mind* (and I paraphrase): "Your spirit is divine...but...your personality remains human and needs the forgiveness of your spirit. As you forgive…you will learn to forgive yourself for all [your] seeming errors."[8]

Forgiveness is an age-old organic requirement. It's a deceptively simple but clearly necessary principle that, although sometimes hard to muster, is a powerfully transcendent and transformative action that's available in any moment, in large ways and small. If you suspect that it's needed, *it is*. It may well be the most important rung on our ladder to personal freedom, because it immediately opens a pathway out of the darkness of victimhood and regret, and lifts us up to a perspective of empowerment, possibility, and hope.

EXERCISE: *Ways of Releasing Real Forgiveness*

As an exercise for discovering forgiveness, notice the next time somebody cuts you off while you're walking down the street or driving in a car. Take a deep breath in and out, and as you breathe out, embody the feeling of letting it go—of *forgiving* and of *being forgiven* for those little indiscretions that we're all guilty of at one time or another. Try to consciously and automatically engage a default of forgiveness every time a resentment pops up in any way. Turn "being offended" into a personal red flag.

As a more serious exercise, sit down for an hour and write down a list of the things you remember that you've done wrong in your life. This will be uncomfortable. It will require self-honesty (that's why that Honesty chapter came first). You don't need to include every little slight; in fact, just a few juicy examples will do. Then enter into those misbegotten experiences in your heart so that you really *feel* their sadness—and *that very sadness will open your heart to forgiveness*.

If you suspect it may be necessary to actually ask forgiveness from the person you've hurt, then it is. You need to act, and you'll find that just mustering the courage to take the action will change you for the better. Then you'll discover what you've always known: that coming

---

8. White Eagle. *The Quiet Mind*, 35.

clean is a beautiful thing, for everyone. If you're not able to apologize in person for one reason or another, *forgive yourself completely* for what you did in the past, and live in a better way from then on, holding on to that feeling to guide your future.

- 6 -
Compassion:
Becoming a Passionate Compassionate

I'm one of those people who thinks we should listen to Tenzin Gyatso, the 14th Dalai Lama, when he says, "Only the development of compassion and understanding for others can bring us the tranquility and happiness we all seek."[9] After all, not only is he a great spiritual teacher and leader, as well as a trans-dimensional spiritual channel to Heaven and all *that* entails, but he's also a refugee from a spiritual mountain homeland that was cruelly invaded and occupied by the forces of material unconsciousness. To deal with such an extreme injustice you need a mountain of forgiveness to embrace a state of total compassion for your oppressors.

While they can't compare to the occupation of Tibet, the challenges of our everyday lives can feel justifiably overwhelming and unfair at times; but if forgiveness is an action for overcoming each obstacle, it's open-hearted *compassion* that provides the real power for the project

We're in This Together
I know I need to constrain my judgmental nature all the time, but if you're anything like me, then the line you get in at the supermarket is always the slowest, the lane you change into on the freeway is the one that suddenly stops moving, and the last piece of your favorite

---

9. The Dalai Lama and Howard Cutler, *The Art of Happiness.*

pie is snatched away just before the plate is passed around to you. In that moment it's very difficult to realize that the person who got that last piece of pie *really loves it too,* and that they're not an adversary or some agent of pain, but that actually the two of you have a lot in common. They'd be very disappointed if they'd missed the last piece too. In that sense you're unified by a kind of "fellowship of the pie," and probably by a whole lot more. Sometimes just the energy in that moment of sudden identification might cause them to inexplicably offer to cut the piece of pie in half and share it with you (or for you to return the favor). Maybe it's the disappointed look on your face that triggers that compassionate concern for your happiness, or perhaps it's just the goodness of their heart. Either way, it's how everything works in Heaven.

Standing in that slow-moving line at the supermarket feels like one of those petty little hells that we all have to endure at times, especially if you're as impatient as I tend to be—but if you could hear what's running through everyone else's head out loud at that moment, it would sound like a chorus of people singing along to the words of a song they all know (set to music): "Why does this always happen to me?" "Don't they know what they're doing?" "Why is the cashier chatting up that customer? Don't they realize I'm in a hurry?" When you realize you're not alone in that silly synchronized mindset, it immediately becomes evident that we're all part of *the same mind,* in a way.

Everyone is going through the same thing here. We all have pretty much the same pleasures, victories, and fulfillments, and the same challenges—the pain, the impatience, the disappointments and losses. We all rise on the tide of youthful energy and slide back into the Source we sprang out of. Although it doesn't necessarily seem like it from "in here," we all respond to these life lessons in almost exactly the same ways, having almost exactly the same thoughts and feelings—often simultaneously—slightly staggered in time by moments, or generations, or centuries.

If we stand back from our Earth and imaginatively assume the perspective from Heaven, it's easy to see how much we all have in common—it's just this view from the ground that makes us think otherwise. It seems to be the self-assigned job of the ego to convince us we're somehow separate from each other when it plainly isn't true. We're all conjoined by human birth and intimately unified by our shared experience of Consciousness, as each of us (and every living thing) perceives it in any given moment. In a way, we're *projections* of one another—aspects of a single being expressed in our unique directions, but still essentially the same thing. We *are* that Divine Single Being.

As we move through life from ambition into meaning, we are making the trip with billions of companion spirits. We might consider the Consciousness we all share so intimately as the language of the angels, and call that language *compassionate* Consciousness. The compassionate atmosphere that angels are enfolded within is, of course, the field of Love.

Thinking Like an Angel Thinks

There's a beautiful 1987 film by German director Wim Wenders called *Wings of Desire*. It's a wonderful imaginary journey into our world down here as angels from Heaven might experience it. They begin each day looking down from very high places like radio towers or office buildings, blending into the statuary. Standing vigil over the human lives below, they determine where they can provide angelic compassion to those most in need of it. They walk among us all the time—on their rounds, as it were. Young children can see them, and the elderly sense their presence with heightened awareness, yet they remain largely invisible, concealed by their cloak of absolute humility. They watch us sleep. They watch us going through hard times. They gently direct us spiritually—direction that either we sense and follow or we don't, depending on how open we are to intuitive guidance. And while no living human they stand next to can actually feel their touch, most of us sense the presence of their love and compassion.

In the film, the angels can hear your thoughts. The contents of your inner dialogue—driven or drifting, wistful, willful, insecure, clever, or *crazy*—are available to them without your outward filter of "self," the way your ego wants to present yourself to others. They know who you really are, because your outsides are only meaningful to them as a projection of your insides. The result is an intensely identifiable, often simply and sadly *moving* experience of life-in-the-moment, shared in the thoughts of each person they listen to.

Imagining this thoughtful scenario supplies us with possibilities for our own realizations. If we could—even for just a moment—assume this angelic perspective, then for just that instant we could identify with both our mortal human thoughts and our angel's penetrating empathy and compassion. We'd witness everyone spending their entire lives trying their best to arrive at the same place in their hearts.

It makes you realize how seeing life from an angel's point of view could clearly expose our poignant shared authenticity—free from ego—and realize that an experience of Love and acceptance is viable in each and every moment. In the eternal moment, we have all the time in the world to become each other.

Then, when we listen to someone speaking (at work, at play, or whenever) and we release the (ego-mind's) need to label their outward appearance and everything they say (their clothes, their opinions, their worries, and the like), we can begin to have an amazingly angelic experience, very much like the angels in the movie. Just *let go* of whether you think you like someone or don't, of whether you think they're brilliant or full of baloney. Release every little bit of judgment that your ego-mind may habitually create. Then, with the freedom granted to you by engaging with compassionate Consciousness, you can gain that momentary control over your unsolicited judgments and simultaneously realize the shared *Self* in all of us. Notice how in that instant your perception of the person in front of you changes, how your feelings toward them *open up*.

Suddenly, their expressions—formed by their life experiences—will arise in that atmosphere of compassionate understanding as they struggle to make you understand them, just as your own expressions sometimes struggle to emerge from you. Intuitively, you may understand that they came from a small town, or from the country, or that they live in a big city. You may imagine very real flashes of their family, their pets, their avocations, and even their dreams. These "imaginary" understandings that seem to arise out of nowhere (without you actually knowing anything about them) are often very accurate. This is the energization of a transpersonal psychic awareness that we are all engaged in, whether we know it or not. (In Heaven, everyone engages in it so intuitively that it's actually how they communicate.)

In Heaven, Time and Space don't exist in the same limited format as human perception allows, so all of this experience of life really can collapse into a single moment of understanding. Opened up to others this way, what you think you're imagining is no longer just your imagination at all, it *is* an extra-sensory, extra-dimensional reality being revealed to you by the transcendent power of compassion.

In Robert Heinlein's wonderful book *Stranger in a Strange Land,* the protagonist is an innocent Martian visitor to our planet, who's able to experience an intensely comprehensive form of empathy and merge with humans he came in contact with. This is the standard state of interaction in greater, shared Consciousness, because everyone (the energy of Heaven *itself)* is engaged in this medium of transpersonal identification, this field of energy that we call *Love.*

As you engage in compassionate Consciousness, and your intuitive identification expands into that single moment, you'll become able to practically see through the other's surface into the authentic self that's struggling to emerge—the internal persona that wants to be seen and heard. The external distinctions and definitions that your ego-mind wants to impose will begin to dissolve, and right there you'll perceive a person's *spirit*—without the designer labels or the great hair or the bad attitude—full of all the expressions and experiences of a life (very much like your own) pouring out of them in every sentence and with every gesture.

Is Your Compassionate Heart Open?

From that very available perspective you will perceive their life to be a lot like your own, because that life actually *is* your own. You'll come to know everyone—from kings and criminals to saints and simple folk—for being who they all really are, for being nearly identical to *who you are too*, in a way. All people, regardless of their title or position, are equal in what amounts to a horizontal hierarchy of billions of souls moving in unison along their particular paths of realization.

Once your heart opens to compassionate insight, it's an easy stroll to experiencing something like an angel's empathy and understanding. None of the petty power struggles or personal peccadillos that normally bother you about any other person need ever bother you again. In fact, you'll witness people more clearly in your heart, and they'll seem almost luminous and outwardly beautiful, regardless of what their physical appearance and demeanor might suggest. Animosities and misunderstandings will fade into a kind of transparency, and without ever actually touching them, people will sense the presence of your Love and compassion. You'll start becoming something of an angel yourself—and needless to say, *that* will take you a long ways toward Heaven. To paraphrase the Dalai Lama, *If you want others to be happy, practice compassion. If you want to be happy, practice compassion.*[10]

This life is a hard life for everyone here, and as you may have guessed, things get a whole lot easier in Heaven…but no one ever said that it would be easy getting there. In fact, in many ways it *has* to be hard for us to find the willingness to engage in spiritual solutions. As is the case with all of these "ladders" to Heaven, they're never deeply understood in any easy way, and finding compassion is no different, especially when we're often walking around life like we're making a movie that we're the star of (that is, that stars our *ego-self*). It isn't possible to write, direct, produce, and star in the

---

10. The Dalai Lama and Howard Cutler, *The Art of Happiness.*

self-made movie of your life unless you are an egomaniac, which makes life a lot harder. If you're the "star" in a movie about yourself, it becomes nearly impossible to witness opportunities for spiritual fulfillment, because you're always too busy acting like "who you are supposed to be" to compassionately witness anybody else. There are plenty of real individuals in Heaven (in fact, everyone experiences their true uniqueness), but they are all *open-hearted* individuals, with fuzzy, overlapping boundaries between one another. That soft-edged open-heartedness—the willingness to engage in compassionate Consciousness—relates directly to your ability to enter the state of calm consideration that is Heaven:

Open heart, *come on in!* Closed heart, *please come back later.*

The Role That Sadness Plays

If you're too caught up in your life (as we always can be) to consider your open-heartedness, there is a guaranteed way that you can find the key to open it; and although it doesn't sound too good, it's such a deep part of human existence that it's often quite comfortable, despite being a little painful. The key to finding compassion in our lives, a key that none of us can avoid finding, is this: *sadness.*

Sadness visits all of us like a long-lost relative whose company we don't always look forward to but then become grateful for in a mysterious but profound way. There's nothing good about it to the outside eye, but inwardly it does make you wonder: *Why is this sad feeling so familiar and strangely appealing?*

It's because sadness opens our hearts (whether we wanted them open or not), and in our search it reliably directs us toward a "secret" passage into Heaven—a small side door that insiders already know exists. Sadness is a magical "sixth-sensory" key into the state of compassionate Consciousness, because it causes us to resonate with structures of the Universe at a deeper level than we normally encounter here on Earth. All of us can realize that kind of deep, shared reality through sadness, and perhaps for some people only through sadness.

Imagine these scenes: the loss of a beloved one to illness or death; the bulldozing of a favorite piece of nature; a favorite childhood milk mug shattered on the floor; the sight of an abandoned pet; the feeling a pop star's song gave you way back when—and the feeling it evokes when that pop star dies; the look in the eyes of a homeless man on the street—and if your eyes meet, how you look into the entire story of a lost life in those eyes, the sad story of a life you might have lived yourself.

Do you feel the sadness in any of those scenes? If you do, then right *now*—in this eternal moment—you are connected to our shared compassionate Consciousness. "You let the pain of the world touch your heart and you turn it into compassion," I've heard it said (probably by a Tibetan Buddhist), and almost nothing more needs to be said about this mysterious gateway into the realm of the heart. Sadness arises within all of us in those places that reveal a great shared meaning. We all know that intuitively; it's just the willingness to use it to explore our compassionate Consciousness that may seem new.

Having Compassion for Everything Alive

It isn't just we humans who live our shared experience within the thin veneer of consciousness that wraps around and enlivens the Earth—it's *all of life on the entire planet*. Notice how difficult it is to consider the cruel fate we mete out to the rest of life on Earth, to all the life of the animal world, without a deep sadness beginning to well up from within. That's because we know exactly what's going wrong. We're being hit over our spiritual heads with it nearly every day. The scenes of animal consciousness we cherish of tenderness and loss, of humor, of loyalty and perseverance—and those of torture and exploitation—score millions of hits on social media channels for one big reason and one reason only: *Animals share compassionate Consciousness with us*, and are in no real way inferior to humans in terms of the connection to our Divine Source. In fact, our deepest sadness comes from knowing that, spiritually speaking, they are even more purely connected than we are.

Animals live simply within their divine, authentic being. Their consciousness is joined with Source purpose and intention, and so they attain a purity of experience within our shared Consciousness through their own uniquely articulated senses and perceptions, which humans seldom even suspect. They've developed capabilities that allow them to live in a richer world than we do, infused by light, sound, smell, air pressure, and electromagnetic waves that connect them to the Divine Field of Being. They aren't burdened by the same convoluted ego-minds as are we humans, so they're effortlessly integrated into nature by their authentic purpose: to live, to love, to enjoy life, and to express their being—all of the same impulses that motivate us.

In fact, the more we learn about animal intelligence, the more we come to realize how animals *think* and *feel* much as we do about kindness, the joys of life and family, and gratitude for the beauty of life. Being simply ignorant or unwilling to compassionately experience the sublimely transcendent intelligence alive in the spirit/mind of a whale or an elephant, for example, our human egos deny all other creatures their true positions in the hierarchy of being, simply because it threatens our ego-sense of self-enhancement and self-importance; and also because it suggests our terminal flaw that has proven fatal to so much of the beauty of the world: the assumption of human "intelligence" that we have the "God-given" right to kill animals for our own purposes and to selfishly exploit Nature—a conclusion based solely on delusion and ignorance, not on necessity or intelligent stewardship.

Indigenous peoples across time have naturally found the way—through the *Great Spirit*—to respectably cycle the energies of hunted and farmed animals while meeting their needs for sustenance. The shared sadness of the sacrifice evokes the compassionate Consciousness they've learned to express as gratitude through myth and ritual. They've demonstrated a deep respect that revered and released the spirits of our animal partners, honored their authentic purpose and connection to the Divine, and then treasured and made use of every part of their mortal bodies.

Few, if any, of these spiritual considerations are shown by our mass culture today. Instead, we suppress this destructive reality and live with the pain of our unconscious behaviors gnawing away at our spiritual and physical well-being and at the healthy viability of our environment.

For us, the sadness, shame, and guilt of our ruthless exploitation of Life on Earth leads to a terminal soul sickness of sorts, especially when we refuse to look at it honestly. It's the real source of inescapable conflict that many people experience in their hearts. Sadly, this sickness disqualifies us from participating in a Paradise that is just within our reach, and that we actually deserve to live in as much as any other creature. We just need to become authentically kind, humble, and honest enough to recognize the source of our sadness and denial—the real consequences of our selfishly destructive behavior—and to transform that sadness into compassionate action. Being in touch with compassionate Consciousness instructs us exactly what to do—and exactly what *not* to do. "Do no harm," the principle called *ahimsa* in Hinduism (and Buddhism) that guided the life of Mahatma Gandhi, is the essential passion and power of compassionate Consciousness.

Imagine Yourself into Compassion

Inspired by sadness, a touch of ennui, or the weight of shame, compassionate direction begins with opening our hearts and freeing our imaginations from the ego-mind that seeks to confine the Divine Spirit alive in the world. It becomes a matter of exercising the kind of compassionate imagination that can help us break out of those bad ego-habits and allow ourselves to make better choices.

One day, walking past a patio café that had been a favorite of the neighborhood for years, I began to grouse about the new ownership that was "branding" it in a more exclusive, upscale way. They'd changed the menu and raised the prices, and the new clientele reflected it. There, in an expensive sedan parked at a red zone in front, was a man in a black suit talking on a cell phone. My ego-mind started jumping to conclusions (the only exercise it gets) about the man's entitled, selfish attitudes when suddenly I had an epiphany: *I didn't know anything about that man, really.* I was imagining the whole story in the part of my ego-mind that specializes in making up fearful stuff.

Then it occurred to me: *What if I just imagined something else?* What if I made up a different story? Why not make up something kind, something good—something *compassionately conscious?*

I decided to invent an equally plausible story about the man wearing the black suit. He was dressed that way because he was a waiter, a regular working stiff. He'd borrowed the expensive car from his boss because his mother was sick and had been taken to the hospital. He was calling his sister so he could arrange to pick her up and take her to the hospital to see their mother. At that moment, the man put down the phone and drove away. I had no idea where he was really going, but in the world of compassionate Consciousness that I had just chosen to experience, that man was no longer a selfish, entitled millionaire, he was a guy a lot like me, on his way to pick up his sister and head down to the hospital. Then I imagined that when they got there, their mother was fine.

My own world instantly became *lighter,* clearer, and more connected. The entire world became easier and more forgiving. I found the perspective that a compassionate imagination can bring to every choice we make in life. It is that perspective from *on high.*

EXERCISE: *Ways of Opening to Real Compassion*

The next time you're having a good personal conversation with someone, try to really become *consciously aware* of them—not just paying attention to what they're saying, but paying *more* attention to it and to the whole experience of them: their gestures, inflections, expressions, and so forth. As you do this, allow your heart to open, and use your compassionate imagination to envision their *being*—expressed in all the nonverbal ways that create their being-in-the-moment.

Try this to bring compassionate Consciousness to the front in your everyday activities—your commute, your errands, your workplace, and the like. As your ego-mind defines your reality at any given moment—as it will do—take over the reins, so to speak. Use your compassionate imagination *to create a new story*, a story of greater sympathy and promise, and then objectively watch what happens in the way you begin to perceive every aspect of your life, and in the way that Life answers you back.

- 7 -
Service:
How You Really Can Meet the Nicest People

As I mentioned earlier, when you start getting closer to Heaven, you'll begin to run into more lovely people (like my old Spanish friend) who'll be happy to stop and give you directions, should you need them. What they're even more likely to do is to drop everything they're doing and insist on showing you the way personally, both to help you and just *for fun*. That's not only because everyone is so kind and compassionate when you get near Heaven but also because it's pretty much what everyone there is always doing: being of service to someone or to something that benefits everyone else. In fact, in Heaven you practically have to ask people *not to help* if you want to do something yourself, and your request will always be respected because everyone will recognize your need to learn something the hard way. Being of service to others and to the common good is just the natural way of doing things there.

It's obvious that being helpful is a good thing and clearly a kind of service to others, but regularly dedicating yourself to the service of others may seem like too much of a commitment than would sit well with your schedule and with your ego. It may seem too time-consuming and even a little *too* humble.

That ought to be the tip-off—because anything that rubs your ego the wrong way usually is the *right* way, and there's really no such thing as being too helpful or too humble, if your intentions are good.

Your unhealthy ego, as usual, is trying to separate you from the tangible benefits of an activity it regards as being "beneath" itself, when, from the spiritual perspective we've gained already, it's clear that our ego is often too low-down to have a decent view. A commitment to service may actually provide us with a loftier, infinitely more realistic point of view—in much the same way that humility can paradoxically be so powerful.

A Misunderstanding of Service

Years ago, when I was beginning my spiritual practice, I went on a spiritual retreat to a beautiful monastery in the mountains where we were waited on hand and foot by a group of nuns who saw to all of the meals and accommodations surrounding our educational sessions. My outlook on life was just beginning to open up at the time, so you could say that I was still a bit "collapsed inward on myself." I was *a bit* self-centered. I had yet to develop much spiritual perspective, despite having had that first out-of-body Near Death Experience. My limited view of my unhealthy ego only allowed me to see the nuns as some kind of victims, as people who had somehow resigned from the realistic demands of life and found a safe place up in the mountains making beds and feeding hungry pilgrims. I felt a little sorry for them, and a little superior to them, but I was also troubled by how happy they seemed to be, and felt like I was somehow missing out on something everyone else understood. That's what a lightly twisted ego can make you believe if you listen to it too closely.

Years later I returned to the same retreat and came under the care of the same group of nuns, only this time I had some years of meditation, study, and service for others under my belt. My healthier perspective showed me a whole new picture of these ladies and the selfless effort they tirelessly contributed to the comfort and well-being of a bunch of strangers. With a naïve admiration, I watched the nuns joyfully tending to our every need, and began to share in this palpable vibration—this tangible divine, purpose-filled energy that they radiated as they went about the business of taking care of us. I witnessed the exhilarating spiritual empowerment that being of service to us was creating in their lives every day.

Then I began to feel a little sorry for the person I'd been the first time I came to the retreat, but having had a little experience being of service myself, I was happily more able to identify with the power that humility gave the nuns. I forgave the old me, and saw that while their efforts made us all comfortable and relaxed and allowed us to enjoy the retreat in a grace-filled way, their work was doing something very real for them too.

Every day they dropped much of what modern life tells us is important in order to simply be of service to others who needed their help. Suddenly it occurred to me: *What a fabulous way to live!* It was then I realized that being of service to others wasn't just the standard of behavior you'd find in Heaven, it was what helped get you there in the first place, and what kept you there every day—as long as you remain willing to lay the "important" stuff aside and live with the honest intention of helping others.

But could getting there really be so simple? Could creating Heaven on Earth just come down to a little simple self-sacrifice for the good of humankind?

Well…*yes*, if it could just *come down* to do that—if that willingness would descend into our lives from somewhere up in a higher, finer plane of being and inspire everybody's behavior in this world. Then something began to sound familiar about my "new" way of thinking. It was starting to sound a lot like the lives of all of the famous prophets and teachers of myth and scripture, who in one way or another professed this philosophy of dedicating yourself to the welfare of others. It sounded familiar because it is a lesson we've all gotten over and over whether we were paying attention or not—a lesson we all carry, deep in our souls.

Why the Resistance to Selfless Service?

Being of service to others (and to the world) isn't an expression of what a wonderful person you are, it's an expression of what wonderful people we all can be. Being of service is an expression of the Divine, of how heavenly life can be when we simply share the spirit of helping one another and all Life on our planet. There's a realization that comes with being of service, a freedom experienced when you think about others, chiefly because it's time when you're not thinking about yourself.

Meanwhile, it's those ego-mind obstacles—including the attitude that service is some kind of special effort, some kind of imposition or sacrifice—that can deprive us of one of life's great spiritual realizations (and empowering sensations). So before you run off and volunteer for some good cause (which I'll definitely encourage you to do later), let's start by examining that hesitance we may experience when we consider "selflessly doing service."

Why wouldn't I happily want to drop my important schedule and volunteer to help someone in need? As usual, where we feel a little discomfort may be the very spot where we need to look. So why would there ever be any unwillingness to do something we all know is so beneficial? Could the problem be my ego, making things conditional again?

We've all been of service to others at some time in our lives, and for many of us it's been a natural impulse, or possibly something we've had to do because it was "our duty." Anyone who's played this role has probably noticed the powerful sense of wholeness that we feel when we've contributed to the well-being of someone else, particularly when nothing was asked in return—when service was entirely unconditional. We've always naturally known that was the right way to go about it, haven't we—to do good deeds, asking nothing in return?

However, we may notice that same happy sensation *wasn't there* when we may have expected some kind of payback, some quid pro quo for our good deed—even if it was just how well it may have reflected on us. Well, here's the way it really works: our greatest spiritual dividends return to us only when no material reward is expected (or received). Like the nuns at my retreat, the angels of any realm act in service to others without *any* selfish motives at all—other than to make it more possible for everyone to share in the experience of the Divine. Being of service energetically includes them in the equation of grace. This is how service benefits everyone *on high.*

For many years I considered myself to be a pretty good guy, and there were few occasions when I wouldn't consider taking time out from my busy schedule to help a friend with something they needed—and I'd show up to help, if I could. I think that many of us share a similar willingness and hear that same calling despite our busy schedules. While that's a great start, it's just not the level of willingness to be of service that helps us find our way to a heavenly state of being—but we can always build up to that slowly, if necessary. We can start with the small things, like being considerate enough to push the door open, lift the heavy thing, hold the elevator, give up our seat to someone in need of it, share a limited resource, or let someone merge into our lane. Those are all excellent entry-level efforts into the spirit of service.

Defuse the Ego to Realize Your Authentic Connection

Pay special notice if you ever become at all resentful when you don't receive the same consideration in return while being of service to others, or if you feel a bit underappreciated. That's the ego twist that needs to be released in order to really free up your spirit. An unhealthy ego likes to keep score of how "fair" or "unfair" life is on this insignificant scale, and may cause you to overlook little openings into the spirit of service. Since Heaven can be found in the little things we do for one another, the smallest ways of being helpful can energize the spiritual properties of charity and fellowship—even at the most mundane levels that we employ them.

Applying even the slightest of conditions to making ourselves of service points out this hitch to us: *Do I {secretly} hope to gain something from doing this service for someone?* Expecting even the smallest payback can taint our best-intended efforts for others. Noticing these tiny expectations can awaken you to defuse your ego and tune in to the vibration of Love that service activates—the real rewards that start to flow for everyone when you're being truly selfless.

The truth is that service is probably *best of all* when it seems inconvenient—and even better when no one even knows about it. That's how we wave goodbye to sneaky self-centeredness and consciously expand our heart until an attitude of concerned service directs our every day as a part of our true nature.

When we do good deeds without any expectation of reward, we fold ourselves into a subtle and powerful medium, the hidden machinery of Life—powered by Love. We open up a remarkable, extra-dimensional world of vast potential, and allow the manifestation of all kinds of wonderful benefits for everyone and all of Life. From small things, like picking up a dropped pen, to big things, like giving up your seat on a lifeboat, all service—no matter its scale—has a real, magical effect. One act of consideration or generosity can cascade into a waterfall of beneficial events, as the energy of Love and compassionate Consciousness pours into the world around us and creates the conditions for divine change to take place. It's the proverbial flap of a single butterfly wing that can become a hurricane halfway around the world. Just a smile to a stranger can be a huge act of service. A single small ice-breaking joke can set loose a chain reaction of Love.

Being of service is just *being who you are as authentically as possible,* and showing up for life with open-hearted generosity and willingness. Just being there, and being willing to do whatever you can do, is enough.

We know why being of service liberates us from the sad constraints of this material world when we look at those in need and realize that anyone can become part of that unlucky crowd at some point in their lives. Life's downturns act as a great leveler, and the elimination of our superficial differences in times of shared misfortune—identifying with those in trouble—is the realm in which selfless service does its most powerfully transcendent work—when we all know what it means to need help.

A hurricane washes away both mansions and shacks. A "bum" (once the president of his own company) may be on the verge of becoming a grandfather, and the gift of bus fare home to his daughter's house may be the modest price of his admission to Heaven. A rich girl who's struggled with addiction discovers that helping another addict in pain brings her riches that come only from selfless service. Our willingness to help one another allows all of us to transcend the desperate sense of separation we experience in a time of misfortune—and even if for just that one moment, *that* will always create Heaven here and now.

We are, and must be, of service to one another because once again, *we are one another.* We must be of service to our Earth, because we *are the life of this Earth*—along with every other living thing on this planet.

The Ways Our Good Works Work

There's a reason why service comes after all of the other rungs in the ladder described in this section. It all comes together like this:

The spirit of service and willingness to participate is a function of our essential *kindness* to one another. Acts of charity, volunteerism, generosity, and sacrifice grow out of that medium of shared consideration, conveyed by the open-hearted humor, acceptance, and willingness that kindness always engenders. After all, why wouldn't you perform acts of kindness—to be of service—when you know how much you appreciate such kindnesses yourself? Kindness is the currency of service.

Being of service is our own most graceful acknowledgment of the power of *humility*—the recognition of our fundamental equality, cloaked in the awkward admission that we may all need help at one time or another. This life is not easy for anyone, and being there for one another is the key to our spiritual survival. We're all compositions of the same magical chemistry, somehow miraculously imbued with this life, whose sense of position and entitlement is an illusion on the heavenly scale of things. We can never be "too important" to help someone out—being of service to the life of the planet *is* how we become authentically important.

Service is real *honesty* in practice. We truly acknowledge the suffering of others and become a spiritual witness to the suffering in the world—and we can't deny that. We know that those in need deserve help, like any of us do when we're down, and we honestly admit when there's something *we* can do about that suffering, even if it's only in our own small way (and especially if we can do more about it than other people can). Passing up the opportunity to be of service is understandable sometimes, but passing it up every time is to lie to yourself about your ability to make a difference and to deprive yourself of the beautiful shared energy of charity.

Informed by that fundamental honesty, being of service gives us the opportunity to show ourselves *forgiveness* and make amends for all the petty little selfish actions we've ever been responsible for: for all the times that we passed by a hungry person who had their hand out, for all the times that we resented having to clean up a little mess made by someone we love, for all the times we selfishly put ourselves first and pretended that it was for the benefit of others. Then, unconditional forgiveness can help us balance and correct our self-inflicted harms; in that way, we're caring for ourselves too. There is no minor offense that everyone isn't guilty of having committed at one time or another, so as we selflessly contribute to our shared cause, we can find forgiveness for failings of any size of others and ourselves. We know that the state of our existence is often completely beyond our control—like when that hurricane blows in (as it always will) and service is our means of helping everyone get through the storm.

In the act of serving others, we become the *compassion* that we hope to receive in our own lives. It's like the understanding and tolerance shown to me by the nuns at my retreat, when I looked at them with my shallow superiority and they just smiled and made my bed anyway. We recognize that the difficult struggle within each of us is one we all face together, and treat each other accordingly and with tenderness, connected by this profound identification. Everyone deserves to have the door held open by some smiling stranger who happens to be in the position to do so.

They're holding open the door to Heaven.

EXERCISE: *Ways to Discover the Real Value of Service*

When you get up tomorrow, try a little experiment. Resolve to be of whatever kind of service, large or small, that you can be. Put that goal in the front of your mind, so that if you see a little mess, you clean it up (even if you didn't make it yourself). If a co-worker has forgotten part of their presentation, try to support them so they can recover. If a stranger is struggling with their hands full, give them an extra hand. If a homeless person asks you for a dollar, give them five—and so forth, all day long. Just be sure you don't take credit for it or mention it to anyone. Do it all anonymously. Don't let your left hand see what your right hand is doing. By the end of the day, notice how you feel, and you'll find that you may feel like doing the same thing again the next day.

Then I recommend that you actually look for a good cause in your community—join a club or cause, keep yourself open to any "coincidental" opportunities, or volunteer in a time of emergency, even if it's just for one day. Show up with no expectations whatsoever; just be willing to do whatever needs to be done. This will be made easier by the people you find there (the nicest people you'll ever meet), and as you work side by side with them, you'll become aware of a tangible energy that they share, a straightforward *let's get down to business* vibe that resonates with Love. When you join in and begin to contribute, notice the actual sensation you experience arising within yourself as you become part of the effort to help, part of a spiritual solution.

When you embark on a path of service, it should come as no surprise to you that you'll literally meet the nicest people in those places where people are thinking less about themselves and more about those who need a little help getting through this thing we call Life. In this way, being of service helps us find an invaluable sense of community as we learn to work for people and with people, joined together by our shared Consciousness.

Then, when you can't be there, notice that slight discomfort you feel when you think of your new brothers and sisters helping people who need help. Chances are you'll miss the energy that grows out of being of service, and want to get back to that special fellowship as soon as you can.

PART II:
PRESENCE

You must live in the present, launch your self on every wave,
find your eternity in the moment.
—Henry David Thoreau, *Walden*

In my second Near Death Experience, in the midst of a brilliant white cloud, I was shown scenes from my life on a mystical, interactive screen that opened up before me. These "life review" episodes didn't play in front of me like old home movies, but instead I witnessed them as though they were packages of data—three-dimensional boxes of life information that I was looking into, or could have entered into and *designed myself*, if I'd had the awareness to do so. The time in which they took place didn't matter, but the quality of timelessness they evoked did. They all could have been yesterday or a thousand years ago, but every scenario felt like *right now*. The most important realization they brought was that I could've participated in each instance in a much more conscious way, with much more presence in the *eternal moment*— had I realized it at the time.

It's only with that *presence* that the opportunity to really appreciate and purposefully participate in our lives is made available within every eternal moment.

A Note on the Translations/Interpretations in Section II

Classical translations of ancient spiritual texts are constantly being augmented and added to as their language begins to feel archaic and as culturally corrected approaches and updates become available. Through the centuries, new translations often amount to *interpretations* of earlier translations, based on the cultural and academic inspirations of their interpreters. The scriptural interpretations I give in part II are based on cross-referencing a number of widely read translations from different time periods, cultures, and academic schools, tailored to bring out the textual nuances of our theme in the most respectful, concise, and accurate manner possible. I don't read Sanskrit, Coptic Egyptian, or Persian myself, nor do I pretend to be a bona-fide scholar of Eastern scripture, but I know what these texts have in common that, for many years, has helped me to find a kind of timeless, universal Heaven in my heart.

To me, the most important thing is to pass along this remarkable content with all of its meaning and intention intact. I offer special thanks to Coleman Barks, who has generously made his beautiful translations of Rumi's poems available for our use.

– 8 –
Finding Presence Now:
It's Always Been Now, and Always Will Be

We all constantly experience a certain ongoing phenomenon in our conscious (or sometimes not-so-conscious) life, and that's the feeling that life doesn't seem all that different now than it ever has. For the most part I feel like I'm participating in life pretty much the same way as I always have. Naturally, my cumulative experiences and changing circumstances inform "who I'm supposed to be" at any given time, but still the experience of moving through this life, looking out through this particular set of eyes, hasn't changed a great deal from my childhood to my present. In fact, most of the time, I don't even feel like *I've* changed very much in the way I witness life, although I know that's not true. I've changed a great deal. My understanding of life—my body and my brain, and in fact all the cells that I am composed of—are in a gradual state of flux, an energetic "data" progression cycling through the material experience of life.

I can think back to when my life seemed different from it is now, or cast my mind into the future and speculate on what may come to be, but still the only direct experience I have is in *this* present moment, where everything I perceive occurs. Haven't you ever found yourself thinking, *I should have been paying more attention to that when it was happening.*

Exploring the principles in practice that can change our *perspective* as we have so far in the previous chapters gently directs us to pay attention to what we pay attention to, and to notice the quality of attention we pay to it. I know that the source of every joy and every regret I've ever had, every plan I'll ever make, and every unfulfilled wish I'll ever hope for arises *within this very moment*. So now we'll focus on *now*—that single most important moment of all—to come to understand how anything can happen in any and every moment we experience with *presence*. Get ready to pay attention!

Our Search for Heaven in the Eternal Moment

Well before Plato and Socrates, the Vedic Upanishads and the teachings of the Buddha delved into our relationship with the real mystery of life—the mystery of Life *in this moment*, the mystery of Consciousness. Following in their footsteps were modern philosophers like Spinoza, Kant, and Schopenhauer, who influenced modern academicians and philosophers such as the Swiss psychologist Dr. Carl Jung, the mythologist Joseph Campbell, the "Eastern" philosopher Alan Watts, and Erwin Schrödinger, the co-founder of modern quantum physics (and "the matrix"). They led to a host of brilliant contemporary spiritual teachers, like the late Dr. Wayne Dyer, or *A Course in Miracles* teacher Marianne Williamson, and the Buddhist-inspired Eckhart Tolle.

All of these philosophers (and many more) explore our mysterious interaction with the eternal or the Divine—the forces and energies at work that constitute an "invisible machinery" running beneath, and through, the normal functioning of Life. In the search for more specific heavens, like Nirvana, Zion, Elysium, Paradise, and so on, we could also say that all religions search for the means to direct our participation in this great mystery of being, and offer wisdom to guide our search for the Divine.

As a near-death survivor, I join others who've experienced an afterlife where consciousness isn't dependent on being alive in the way we usually think of it. For us, the existence of eternal life is an ever-present reality. The eternal isn't some infinite expanse of time, it's a measure of the quality of being we find in the present now, a measure that our lives expand into. This is Life *in the eternal moment*—the moment we are always living in, especially when we're paying attention. The more presence we have within each eternal moment, the more conscious awareness we can bring to bear to experience and direct our lives.

Our search for the Source—for Heaven right now—has less to do with following a definitive belief system or school of thought and much more to do with this personal sensory exploration—seeking out enough *presence* in each moment to benefit from what Life is showing us. It's an investment in the way we think about each moment.

It's easier to understand this weighty stuff about *now* if we consider the everyday times when we've got no problem with being present. For example, consider how much you enjoy every bite of your favorite meal (huevos rancheros with black beans, guacamole, and fresh tortillas on the side) and that moment of concentration you bring to the way it tastes, or the intention you bring to listening to your favorite music (*Listen to this—this is my favorite part!*). Relishing the moment when a child achieves some special honor, or drinking in a truly spectacular view, or appreciating great sex—there's no problem being fully engaged in those moments, without hardly even giving it a thought. You're fully present and able to appreciate the moment so well that you wish you could save it or extend it, and you can with what the Buddhists call *mindfulness*—that is, living each moment in a state of conscious awareness, as much as you possibly can, so that those life experiences register deeply in your soul.

Presence allows us to learn the lessons we learn only in the *eternal* moment, not in the *external* moment. We gain a spontaneous understanding of this when we unexpectedly experience something beautiful, or in the moment when we suddenly feel the unexpected relief of forgiveness, or when we need to be immediately present for a friend in distress—when what's needed is just to pay attention! These moments have an entirely different quality than those when our lives are on cruise control, when we skim along the surface from one passing expectation to another. While it's impossible to maintain the constant concentration necessary to completely immerse ourselves in every moment, cultivating the most authentic level of engagement we can is the only way to properly pay attention to what might be important—even if it doesn't seem important at the time. Lots of times we don't even know what we may be missing.

The Perspective of Presence

Maintaining presence allows us to respond appropriately to life's personal challenges. Our ego always wants to be in control by labeling, judging, comparing, and making demands, while being truly present lets us recognize our harsher ego demands and reject them, allowing our deeper, intuitive intelligence to arise within that eternal moment. If we let our ego-mind—our feeling offended, our sense of injustice, our need to be right—spontaneously dictate our actions, we tend to be *reacting*, or often *over*-reacting, to simple circumstances. We can blow situations out of proportion, losing the perspective that kindness, humility, honesty, forgiveness, and compassion can give us. In fact, we can make proper choices only when we're fully present to do so, because not only does presence give us the priceless gift of constraint—the ability to take that extra moment to let sanity and reason arise—but it also puts us in touch with an existent intelligence that is greater than our own. Just stopping and intently focusing on one breath can instantly allow us to check in with Heaven, so to speak.

In Heaven nobody gets caught overreacting in senseless or destructive ways. Everyone relishes taking that eternal moment to adjust to every situation. In fact, in Heaven everyone is quite calm and thoughtful, as you may have already imagined.

We can also see how presence works in the focus we bring to our everyday efforts in life, great and small, such as raising our kids, doing our job, preparing a meal the very best we can—why, even folding our t-shirts just so (*doesn't anyone notice how well I do this?*). On a grander scale, presence is in the plans we make to realize our future and to accomplish our dreams. In any effort where we want to be successful, we know we can't be all over the place and really be effective—we have to be present right *here* and *now*. We have to focus our intentions to move ahead with intelligent purpose.

In an appropriately metaphorical way, we're completely present when we plan and plant a garden. As we plant seeds in a row, we picture what they'll look like as they grow, how we'll tend to them until maturity, and even how we're going to cook them up after harvest and how fresh and delicious they're going to taste.

This is how presence affects our *karma,* the cause and effect of our essential life actions, as well as what lies at the magical heart of intention and spiritual methods for manifesting. We engage with a deeper reality by focusing the present on what the outcome can be. Anything can happen in this miraculously plastic life, and using your imagination to picture the end result you desire, banishing negativity, having *faith* in the constant, creative force at work in Life, and *supplying the effort* is the process that's always available to us in any moment. In this way, with conscious awareness we can bring our dreams into reality by directing our intentions with presence. We plant seeds in this moment. We know how well they can grow. We pay attention to how well they're doing and to what we want them to become. *We are the stewards of their becoming.*

Presence Leads to Faith

Presence asks us to pay attention to something bigger too. The real reason for its effectiveness is because it asks us to rely on the *faith* that we are participating in a greater reality. It's the reality where we usually find that in this very moment everything is really okay and everything is possible—just the way it is now. We find the truth that right in this moment *I am* safe and taken care of (and apparently always have been) in a way I can't acknowledge unless I'm fully present to realize it. Presence provides a grace that allows us a kind of personal default, a reset button, out of our momentary difficulties and back into a reality of infinite possibility and limitless Love.

Faith is not always a well-lit place, but with presence your eyes get used to the dark. A light begins to shine into dark corners, and you begin to perceive more of the illumination that's available to you if you ask for it. "Now faith is the substance of things hoped for, the evidence of things not seen,"[11] the New Testament mysteriously suggests. It isn't a heartless darkness out there after all, but the field in which *prayer* actually lives and thrives. In moments of intense presence—maybe when all else seems to have failed us—we turn inward to cast a prayer out there, into the radiance where our angels are listening. We all know the personal intensity of those moments, and that special, powerful presence we bring to bear then. That simple, powerful energy of prayer can reveal a miraculous resource to us, and focusing those prayers for direction can be a regular practice that we don't need to save only for special occasions.

As we recognize presence in everyday moments, we realize there's a connection that grows if we practice these private rituals every day. As faithful participants in an eternal reality, through prayer and meditation we can open those passageways to the shared intelligence that's alive in those moments of transcendent being. Prayer (asking Heaven) and meditation (listening to Heaven) are the very best ways to tune our brains to the frequency of the Divine, and to discover our life's authentic purpose.

The Endlessness of a Moment

In my second Near Death Experience, I entered a kind of cloud where I was shown these intensely meaningful (preferably forgettable) moments from my life. I was forced to be completely present for those moments again, where I could have learned something important or could have been something more for someone else. I remember those moments with more clarity than most of the other memories I've had, and you'll hear that a lot from Near Death Experiencers—that their NDE memories have a different quality than the memories they've had before. I believe that's simply because of the quality of presence in that eternal reality, unconstrained by our external, physical bodies. There's a much more illuminative focus in the experience

---

11. Hebrews 11:1.

free of our limited senses. It's the result of a total, unfettered engagement in Divine Consciousness.

What were those memories like, and what did they tell me about the invisible machinery at work in this world? Each scene wasn't made up of cascading or flashing fragmentary images, like most of my memories. Instead, they were like discrete, dimensional panels—3-D boxes of time, in a way—that I could almost step into and relive again. They had an enhanced quality of real life in the eternal moment, rather than the bits and pieces I may rearrange to suit a story of myself that my ego wants to tell—the quality of the present timeless dimension that we're all living in. I experienced all the sensations of real joy and real loss (both!) activated within each momentary box of time, as well as a sense of control—an ability to design and direct the "life data" alive in those moments. It was a sense of understanding and empowerment that only my bodiless presence could reveal to me.

Since then, I haven't been able to pass by any moment too lightly—I realize that matters of great consequence can crop up anywhere, at any time. There are people (even complete strangers) who need to be listened to, and situations that require my attention and perhaps my participation—even if they're unexpected, and even if I'd rather be somewhere else. With my newly inspired faith, those unexpected boxes of time began to open up in miraculous ways, revealing unforeseen powers and possibilities. They led me to new paradises that I could have easily lost but instead were presented to me—even when I didn't feel that I deserved them.

This expanding perception of what's possible began to demonstrate to me that the invisible machinery of Heaven is at work in every moment, everywhere you may happen to be looking, if you are present to witness it.

Manifesting Consciousness in Presence

In the years since the discovery of one of science's most reliable theories, the theory of quantum mechanics, we've had to come to terms with the idea that we function as a part of a pretty magical kind of reality, scientifically. We've had to consider the idea that we live in an "observer-based reality" where reality appears to us through our powers of consciousness—a kind of cosmic awareness that we've all entered into by simply having been born into this form of energy that we call *human,* interacting with all the other energetic forms of the Universe.

As a person who has experienced that Consciousness is separate from my body, as a *field of being* that exists without boundaries rather than as a phenomenon being formed by my brain every instant I'm awake (and in some weird ways when I dream), the idea that reality is created within a big, benevolent field of intelligence doesn't seem unusual to me at all. The Universe is full of miracles, and the mystery of Consciousness is probably the hardest one of all to comprehend, much less to control, but perhaps all we're ever really called upon to do is to relax and allow the miracles of Life to reveal themselves.

Realizing abundance in life may have less to do with mastering new techniques to create material results than with simply witnessing how you already work in this big luminous picture of Life, in every moment. The problem with some techniques of manifestation is that you can end up with your demanding ego making you feel like you're not doing it right. In truth, the most successful practitioners of "magical" life skills are people who've almost entirely given up any attachment to anything material, people who possess a simple, spiritual perspective on life, authentically grounded in every moment. The kind of success we think of as heavenly really has very little to do with mastering obscure secrets and a lot to do with willingness and our conscious participation in every moment of Life. We don't find it by wishing for it—*it finds us* when we live our life with the intention of being present for the miracles that are happening all the time.

Synchronicity and the Timeless Now

Many people have an idea of what the term *synchronicity* means in popular use, but in a lot of cases they confuse it with the simple idea that occasionally we all experience timely coincidences. We've all had it happen to us—those accidents that seem as though they were by design; but the concept of synchronicity as proposed by the great Swiss psychologist Dr. Carl Jung removes most of the accident from the accidental nature of coincidence. He suggested that a coincidence is only the visible tip of a profoundly synchronistic iceberg, so to speak—the doors to a glass-bottom boat that occasionally open to reveal a hidden living order operating beneath the surface of things— evidence of the interdimensional, interlocking "boxes of experience" that I experienced in my second Near Death Experience.

Dr. Jung's original version of synchronicity pointed out the presence of certain recurrent images and ideas, *archetypes*, in these remarkable happenstances: in dreams that seem to come true, timely meetings, omens that accurately predict the future, signs that bear great significance in our personal experience, and the like. Moments of intense and meaningful coincidence are often foreshadowed by images such as icebergs, pearls, butterflies and birds, crosses and circles (of life), mysterious boxes of fate, or the appearance of an unusual stranger. These poetic archetypes pop up in our lives and direct us into an unseen, benevolent world of conscious understanding where our answers can be found, and where we can discover how our authentic selves actually fit right in—a process he called *individuation*.

Dr. Jung didn't feel the need to go out on a limb and define these new principles because he was a crackpot mystic, but because after years of presence working with patients, of studying scripture and mythology, and by bearing witness to the events, travels, and discoveries of his own life, it became clear to him that there really did appear to be a mysterious, underlying kind of connecting "field" in effect throughout one's life experience. "Synchronicity is an ever present reality for those who have eyes to see," Dr. Jung supposedly said (perhaps a bit mischievously).[12]

Not coincidentally, at the same time the world was first becoming aware of the theory of quantum mechanics and the concept of a *quantum field* from which all matter arises; that it's actually our presence,

---

12. Jung, *Synchronicity: An Acausal Connecting Principle.*

consciously engaging in that field—our focused attitudes, intentions, and actions—that synchronously interact to create our reality. So it made sense that Dr. Jung would refer to this synchronizing field as *unus mundus*—a unified world—and its connecting mechanism as *synchronicity*, the principle by which our personal and collective experience is connected to our shared Source.

With the mind of an academician attempting to describe a deeply spiritual process, Dr. Jung based the material reliability of his synchronistic model on three aspects of mostly spiritual potential: *meaningful coincidence*—that coincidental happenstances seem to happen sometimes with very specific, personal meaning; *causal connection*—that despite there being no apparent material cause, these events have a profound personal significance that demonstrates an intentional connection of some kind; and *luminosity*—the indication that all of this happens within a kind of shared field of divine light-based energy, in communion with a greater state of transcendent illumination (as described throughout history).

The Luminosity of Everything Now

I bring all of this up now because synchronicities are occurring in our lives all the time (in fact, you could set your watch by them in Heaven), but without presence they're bound to go unnoticed. It's presence that reveals these mysterious connections to us—not as coincidences, but as the way things actually work in between the dual natures of our material and spiritual lives. Presence allows and inspires this luminosity to grow into a powerful capability, part of a sixth-sensory awareness that opens up a whole new world of possibility for us. Engaging in the eternal moment with our principles of spiritual perspective can expand this luminous nature of our perceptions, and we can actually begin to *see* the light streaming through the forms of Life.

All of Life really does radiate with energy in the same classic sense that we picture Heaven to be a place of luminescence. We experience this luminosity *in the moment* as the light shining from within certain people, or in the transcendent beauty of some natural phenomena. Being human, we can only see the tip of the luminous iceberg, but we can have faith that the rest of it stretches deep beneath the surface of what we can see, illuminating unseen possibilities. In her wonderful book *Illuminata,* Marianne Williamson puts it this way:

> Our own luminosity...prepares the ground for positive materialization....The luminous mind has a quantum effect. It doesn't have a practical influence in ways the world can always see....Luminosity is our miracle-readiness....Luminosity is the power of the mind to influence the world in a positive way.[13]

Our experiencing *this* moment in our life informs us of a profoundly common truth: that *this* is how it's always been—that *now* is when it's always happening. The presence of living in this life— always in this eternal moment—indicates that the experience of living hasn't been much different for anyone, all throughout the ages. The circumstances surrounding us, the intelligence we share, the "progress" of civilization and culture, the advance of technology, the exploitation and degradation of Earth's ecosystems—all of these aspects of life continue to change, but the experience in the eternal moment remains unchanged, like a rocky river bottom as the world of changing phenomena rolls over it.

There's a tendency on our part to believe that we know more now than we ever have, and while it's true in a way, life's deepest realizations haven't necessarily found their ultimate expression in lockstep with human "progress." Since *now,* eternally, has always been *now,* every deep observation made about human experience throughout history is continuously valid, and applies with equal weight to the quality of human life in any era.

Up until my second Near Death Experience, I didn't have much appreciation for the life experiences of others, much less the currency

---

13. Williamson, *Illuminata: A Return to Prayer,* 26–27.

of wisdom that had accumulated over time. Years after my second NDE, when I finally broke down my boundaries through surrender and meditation, every moment of recorded existence became a new frame of reference for me, and suddenly—completely unexpectedly—the world of wisdom scripture and spiritual literature came alive for me in ways I never could have imagined. From that point on, I began to hear the voices of the ancients as though they were talking directly to me.

Discovering Our Presence in the Past

Since everyone has always experienced life *in this same way*, every piece of "ancient" wisdom ever set down about the way life works is a valid description of what we're all going through in this very moment. Socrates, the Buddha, Jesus, or Saint Teresa—or any other wise, transcendent spirit—walked around in a body not all that different from the one we have now, equipped with a mind not all that different from ours.

Fortunately for us, all of that profound transcendent understanding is still available through ancient scriptures and wisdom teachings that many of us may have overlooked, thinking they couldn't possibly apply to life today. But Truth is timeless, and it's good to remember that teachers from the past didn't have the distractions that our over-developed sales-driven mega-culture constantly imposes on us. They spent their entire lives in deep contemplation and experimental experience without having to deal with the invasive complexities of modern life (no TV!). As a result, their observations speak to us with clarity and precision, capturing and describing levels of existence that are avoided and even suppressed nowadays—largely because their direct spiritual power threatens the compromised values forced on us over many years of technological reconditioning and corporate media influence.

Our highly technological culture of today looks at life as a kind of series of material coincidences, but Heaven is not of a material nature at all—it is spiritually present within everyone and everything. While our modern technological connections are very real, the deeper realities described by the ancient sages detail our involvement in a form of *spiritual technology*—an authentic underlying conscious field that truly connects us in every instant, that never changes with public opinion and never goes dark when its battery dies or the power goes out. That can make all the difference when you're deciding which connections are eternally more important than others.

A good case could be made for the idea that as a species blessed with (or cursed by) complex thought, we've actually been devolving in a way since the invention of writing and printing (and especially TV) became popular. Before that, all of the accumulated wisdom of human experience was passed down orally—memorized with astounding accuracy and reverence for the wisdom alive in the teachings.

Within this very moment it's possible for us to reclaim this collected wisdom as our own, because this moment isn't exclusive at all—it's where we can free ourselves from the constraints of Time as a linear, biological reality and simultaneously experience everything that has ever been experienced and will ever be experienced. In the next chapter we'll spend some time with four ancient guides to Heaven and the different ways they pass their profound insights along: from the narrative metaphor of the Hindu *Bhagavad Gita,* to the mind-science of the Buddha's *Dhammapada,* to the Zen-like mystic myth of the Gnostic *Gospel of Thomas,* and culminating with the transcendent poetry of Jalal ad-Din Muhammad Rumi. We'll make an effort to find our path to Heaven by way of the accumulated awareness of these great teachers, as well as being assured that there's plenty more timeless wisdom where that came from.

I'd also invite you to look into texts like the *Upanishads,* Plato's *Phaedrus,* Lao Tzu's *Tao Te Ching,* Patanjali's *Yoga Sutras,* Shankara's *Crest Jewel of Discrimination,* William James's *The Varieties of Religious Experience,* and Walt Whitman's *Leaves of Grass,* as well as *The Cloud of Unknowing, Pirkei Avot,* the *Gospel of John,* and so very many more that reveal the same truths—the same directions to Heaven—expressed in slightly different ways. Aldous Huxley, the twentieth-century author of *Brave*

New World, described four principles and realizations common to all of these truth-seeking disciplines in his book *The Perennial Philosophy*. These principles describe what may be common to any of our concepts of Heaven:

1. First, the material world, through the nature of our consciousness, arises out of a Divine Field of Being in which all realities exist. That perspective is the field in which Heaven is experienced.

2. Second, human beings can't know the Divine by presumption, but only through a direct form of inner experience. That presence is the means through which we experience Heaven.

3. Third, our human-being comprises a *duality*—consisting of our outward, ever-changing material self and ego-mind; and our inner Self, or "divine spark," that is always connected by its true nature to Divine Consciousness.

4. And lastly, we're here to recognize the transcendent part of our self that is actually alive in Heaven. We're here on Earth to identify our authentic selves with this eternal reality—that is our essential purpose.

You'll notice that all of these principles described by Mr. Huxley are functions of right *now*—alive in the instant when human consciousness expands into the Divine. That transformative moment can be described by the archaic idea of *alchemy*—not as the process that transmutes lead into gold, but as a metaphor for the means by which simple matter is brought to life by Divine Consciousness.

I believe that miracles can be experienced in any moment, particularly when you sit in nature, open your eyes and *your heart,* and witness the light pouring through the trees, bouncing off the snow, shining in the eyes of any animal, oozing out of great boulders, and perched on a glowing hillside. Everything is alive and radiates its own energy in the eternal moment of that realization. Then everything alchemically, energetically, turns to "gold."

The perception of this divine light energy applies to people too—it's why some people seem to shine, while others seem dense and troubled. In any moment, people can take on the nature of low-vibrational thought-matter and seem down or blue, while warmer and livelier people appear to be lit up from within and are actually vibrating closer to the frequency of Source energy. Presence allows the open-hearted awareness of these energies, sensory changes in vibration, and the perception of the actual "glow" of Source energy pouring through us.

Understanding, identification, and compassionate Consciousness grow out of this way of looking at life. In the heavenly eternal, these energies are modulated within the higher, balanced frequency called *Love*.

It's really only through presence that we witness the Love streaming or struggling, the light energy waxing and waning through the physical forms of life, and truly recognize the eternal in one another, and the obstacles that may obscure it. This real nature of reality can be appreciated only through presence, where you also know that these perceptions are a reflection of your own state, your own vibrational energy. Life *is* a mirror. How you feel (the frequency of your thought-forms) actually elicits your experience of the world, and in that way you are constantly creating your own world. Life is a continuum, lived in the present.

EXERCISE: *Entering into Presence*

A simple exercise for realizing your immediate sense of presence could start as a kind of meditation (which we'll go into more thoroughly later on) and evolve into what we might call a prayer. It goes like this:

Sit comfortably, with your eyes closed and your head slightly bowed. Relax and breathe in and out, deeply and easily. Hold your hands in front of you, palms down, and open your eyes. Carefully observe the backs of your hands in detail. Turn them palms up, and closely examine their remarkable structure—the incredible engineering of bone and tissue and blood vessels—and their miraculously sensitive mobility. Keep your palms up, lift your head, and take in your surroundings, fully realizing the space around you. Then close your eyes, deeply breathe in the material space you occupy, breathe out your surrender into the mystery, and offer out loud something like this:

> *Thank you, Universe, for this very moment of Time in which I am alive.*
> *Help me to be constantly aware and realized within this body, within this space, with this presence toward all that I encounter.*

Breathe in and out deeply once more, then open your eyes slowly and witness the light energy streaming out from every direction.

I'd also like to offer you an exercise for activating your presence that's pretty simple and fun and that I think you'll find quite effective:

Make this coming week an "open-hearted week," where you try your best to experience your life with as much conscious awareness in each moment as you possibly can. When you forget to, just generously push "reset" to really pay attention to your surroundings, to listen carefully to others, and to try and witness *the light* entering into your eyes through the forms of people and experiences you're perceiving. Do this the very best you can, and watch what happens, as you'll actually begin to see in a different way—with a balanced perspective, focused in the moment, and witnessing the illumination pouring through the miracles (from a bus stop to the Grand Canyon) that surround us every day.

– 9 –
The Presence That Lasts:
Uncovering Ancient Paths to Heaven

Any historian will tell you that our stories are timeless, only the names and wardrobes keep changing over time—that's why we can always experience real identification with stories of individual struggles. It's because they carry fundamental principles of a deeper reality dressed in their historical context, whether the story is from last week or from a very long time ago. The great mythological narratives are timelessly alive, passing along lessons from the past, providing us with symbolic insights into the nature of our very existence, and inspiring the transformative passages into purpose and joy we may think of when we think of what Heaven can be.

The unforgettable experience to be had sitting at the foot of a sage "old soul," a respected elder, or sometimes a surprisingly youthful purveyor of what's clearly profound wisdom is always the same whether you're wearing an animal hide, a tunic, a sari, or a pair of blue jeans. I don't remember what I was wearing—or even if I actually *had a body*—when I learned the lessons of my three Near Death Experiences, only that I was inhabiting that eternal moment when all the greatest lessons can be learned, if we're paying proper attention. The words of the prophets and great teachers carry that timeless beneficent impact—we are lovingly hit over the head, held by the heart, and changed forever, struck softly and deeply by their myth, their logic, and their poetry.

The following are just four brief examples of such timeless, transformational teachings.

The Bhagavad Gita: A Peaceful Battle to Find Heaven

Out of all my favorite tales of spiritual symbolism, one that speaks directly to our goal is the tale of the *Bhagavad Gita,* a gem plucked from the middle of the vast Hindu historical epic the *Mahabarata.* The Gita (as it's known for short) is nothing less than a comprehensive guidebook for discovering self-purpose, unification with Divine Being, and an approach for acquiring unshakable happiness. It's metaphorically disguised as a battleground saga where symbolic forces of good and evil clash and issues of inner and outer life-or-death are being decided at every moment and for all time. This ancient document that many may dismiss as being a little out-of-date is actually a very up-to-date, life-shaping owner's manual—a guide to the inner search for a higher reality alive in everything we see and in everything we can be. In short, it's a handbook for finding Heaven, concealed within a remarkable story of duty and conquest.

What We Fight to Find Heaven

Our personal avatar in the tale of the Gita is an incomparable archer and warrior named *Arjuna,* pitted against his blind uncle and his ambitious son whose forces include his beloved family members, old acquaintances, and favorite life-teachers—all bent on controlling a kingdom that (metaphorically) stands for the realm of inner peace and eternal happiness we're all looking for. The "battleground" is the field where the struggle for our own personal heaven takes place, against those parts of ourselves and our personalities (our "cousins and teachers") that we've always relied on but who now may betray us by creating obstacles between us and our own fulfillment. They're conflicts caused by the persistent lack of perspective and presence that tend to obstruct us or sabotage our own path to happiness. But who, if anybody, could possibly help us negotiate such a rocky road to Heaven? For that quality of guidance we'd need a very well-qualified driver.

In order to concentrate on shooting his arrows, Arjuna has a charioteer who happens to know his way around this perilous ground intimately well. His driver just happens to be *Krishna*—the personification of God on Earth—and just before the battle when our hero understandably gets cold feet, Krishna stops and gives him the greatest pep talk of all time on how the Universe works *from God's point of view*. It's not a bad perspective to have shared with you firsthand. Krishna proceeds to give Arjuna detailed directions on exactly how to navigate the path to Heaven (about life's hidden spiritual machinery), and how, as struggling passengers ourselves, *we too* can most effectively overcome our obstacles and attain the peaceful, unified state that Hindus call *moksha*.

A Basic Map of the Gita's Heaven

In the Universe of the Gita, the infinite, indivisible ground of all being is called *Brahman*. It's what physicists may call the "unified field," or what I like to call Divine Consciousness. It is the all-embracing field of creation that you may prefer to call *God*, if you please. Absolutely *everything* is Brahman, and *everything* is spirit, and so *everywhere* really can be Heaven. Our personal spiritual connection to Brahman—what we would usually think of as our soul or spiritual self—is called *atman*. Realizing the personal union with that luminous field of creation is the experience Hindus call *samadhi*.

Yoga, in the Gita, isn't only like the *hatha yoga* so commonly (and commendably) practiced as a form of physical meditation, but is actually a group of disciplines that can reconnect us to Heaven. They're different approaches that lead to the same place, practiced as *Jnana yoga*: the way of the intellect; *Bhakti yoga*: the way of devotion to, and identification with, the Divine Source; *Karma yoga*: the practice of selfless service to others; and *Raja yoga*: a combination of all of those disciplines, centered around the practice of meditation.

A couple more important Vedic concepts that you've likely heard of are *dharma*, which are the laws that describe and connect all the working parts of Life (the invisible machinery, so to speak), and *karma*, which we've all experienced as the cause-and-effect nature of life experience. Dharma is the proper way to live, while karma is simply the *actions* that lead to results and reactions—even though we all mostly understand it as "What goes around, comes around." Our karma is the "data" packet of collected experience we create that informs both our external and our eternal lives—accumulating and transferrable from life to life—as we slowly learn how to shape ourselves to better reunite with Brahman. (We can align ourselves with dharma and create better karma for ourselves when we practice the principles that improve our perspective on life, namely kindness, humility, honesty, forgiveness, compassion, and service.)

The Divine Advice of the Gita

By now you're probably wondering what, exactly, did God have to tell our hero? As Arjuna begins to voice his fears about destroying everything he's come to depend on in life, Krishna calms him down and puts his human worries into the larger context of Life, from God's perspective:

> Everything that changes is not real; reality exists in the unchanging eternal. Those who experience both live in the truth. Recognize the eternal that pervades the universe and realize the indestructible nature of eternal life. The human body lives and dies, but the true Self is immortal and limitless—so fight the battle!
> —Bhagavad Gita, II:16–18

Immediately we learn that to deal with life's hardships comfortably we've got to realize our spiritual perspective. Everything is always changing and shifting in this world, and the true nature of our human form is impermanence. Our growth and acquisition of status and possessions are always followed by some degree of inevitable decline. People, things, and opportunities—all forms of expression "live" and "die" around us constantly. Beliefs that we've relied on may turn into obstacles, and only their "defeat" allows new realizations to grow and enrich our lives. The Gita encourages us to lose our attachment to whatever we *thought* we needed and to become entirely willing to rid ourselves of old habits that obstruct us from a more rewarding experience of life.

Being any kind of warrior is never easy, whether you're an ancient archer or a struggling present-day entrepreneur, so allowing Krishna to "drive your chariot" makes the battle much easier to win when you only have to concentrate on your part. We can paint ourselves into hellish little corners by trying to assume too much control over the mysterious forces at play in our lives, but we actually *gain* power by relinquishing the idea that we can always control them.

This is where the Bhagavad Gita gets specific about how the invisible machinery of Heaven really operates in this world: if we can't control what happens in our lives, what are we supposed to be doing here? We have to do *something* to create the quality of life that we want, don't we? But Krishna suggests that there's a particularly counterintuitive approach to getting to where we want to be: *Do what you do as well as you can, and don't worry about the results.* The implication is that Krishna will do the driving for us—especially if we're living in a basically positive way:

> You have the right to act to the best of your abilities, but not to expect any personal reward for it. Never take action only for selfish motives, or fail to take action when no reward is promised. Perform your work established within your spiritual Self—free from competition or selfish desires. Self-realization lies in a balanced mind.
> —Bhagavad Gita, II: 47–48

While it may not seem possible that a suggestion like "do your best without any expectations for the results" can empower us on the battlefield of life, the enemies we face—the obstacles we create—almost always come from fears for the future and regrets from the past—from *not living in the moment*. Releasing the grip of our selfish expectations allows us to project faith and intention into our lives, and by focusing with presence in the moment, our best efforts will create our reality—all the while depending on a deeper reality to actually supply the ultimate results. And this takes place in an atmosphere of grace and gratitude, because instead of always having to work so hard against the current, we can simply allow faith and the benevolent flow of the eternal to carry us toward our goal.

In teaching us *how things really work here*, Krishna directs us toward a different kind of success than that of our insistent material demands—free from the realm of self-gratification that comes and goes, leaving us hungry for more. Real success comes from simply *allowing* yourself to live in Heaven, not from struggling to get what you want.

On top of that, the Gita teaches us about the nature of the Self in all things, and the reality of our shared divinity that needs to be recognized, respected, and celebrated—just as the occupants of Heaven recognize the eternal in everything, and regard the obstacles created by self-centeredness as their enemies on the inner battlefield. They experience Love as the Unified Consciousness in all creatures, in all people, and in all the natural processes of the Universe they themselves are part of:

Free from pride, violence, arrogance, anger, the lust to control and to possess; having lost all sense of "mine," one finds peace in the authentic self. Joyfully connected to the Divine, beyond desires and regrets, and with a deep connection to all Life, Love unites one with the Source of all, and through the grace of selfless action, one enters into Heaven.
    —Bhagavad Gita, XVIII: 53–56

Throughout its remarkable course, the Bhagavad Gita remains a very reliable map to Heaven that will never need to be redrawn—a document of great compassion, wisdom, imagination, and intelligence, and one of timeless history's most inspiring and comprehensive guidebooks to the invisible machinery of human existence.

Buddhism: Going From Nervous to Nirvana

Everyone knows a Buddhist or two. That's because there are a lot of Buddhists in the world, and more all the time. Perhaps Buddhism is gaining so much popularity as a life approach because in this chaotic world of shifting values and technological change, its teachings defuse life's urgent demands and supply us with a reliable source of tranquility—call it a "spiritually scientific" strategy for survival. The result is that the Buddha's insights may be even more meaningful for us today than they were 2,500 years ago, when he began his mission to awaken the world. And since Buddhism is not really a religion (as the Buddha designed it), but is actually a kind of science-of-the-mind, so to speak, a person of any faith may adopt it as a tranquility-enhancing practice.

The Buddha's realm of Heaven, or *nirvana,* is a state of being that can be approached by anybody willing to follow a set path, grounded in the practice of meditation. Its course leads us through the quality of our perceptions, toward the cessation of self-induced suffering, into compassionate acceptance of the world "as it is," and realizing the loving identification with all Life which culminates in a sincere desire and effort to bring everybody else along too. Like a "science of the transcendent," Buddhism provides us with a kindhearted and scrupulously well-reasoned methodology to ease our suffering and conflict, a revolutionary approach to living he based in the fundamental lessons he called the *Four Noble Truths:*

1. Life is full of suffering.
2. There are understandable causes of all of that suffering.

3. If our suffering can be understood as how we perceive and think about life, then that means we can find solutions for it the same way.

4. There's a surefire program that can be followed to put those solutions into effect—a kind of route to Heaven that Buddha called the *Eightfold Path*.

You'll notice we've already got four Noble Truths and an Eightfold Path, and that's really just the start of it. When you enter into the vast content of the Buddha's teachings, you'll find that there are lots of lists—structure that's needed to methodically explore and understand them all. The Buddha was truly the world's first great depth psychologist—an inner explorer without peer, who miraculously realized practically *all* the motivations that make us want what we want, do what we do, and feel the way we feel—and as a result, what all the best variations are for directing our lives toward happiness and fulfillment.

A Brief Bio of the Buddha

In terms of the world we live in, many of us lead fortunate lives, but not many of us have a life like the Buddha did. He was born around 550 BCE as an Indian prince who really "had it all." The heir to a kingdom of great wealth and power, raised in a cloistered court of privilege and luxury, he eventually discovered the essential common truth about living in this world—that this is obviously a life of great potential suffering. After years of taking a vow of abject poverty and contemplative austerity, he realized that the only possible way to escape the grip of life's inevitable sufferings must lie in a balanced "middle path" between the extremes of lack and excess. He discovered that it was only by comfortably focusing directly into the middle—into his own present moment of experience—that he could find a release from fearful suffering and the realization of bliss.

The practice of deep meditation was critical to the Buddha's effort, for as he silently sat and explored the inner structure of being itself, freed from the activity of thought, he found an effervescent solution that dissolved his sense of separateness and the constraints of human suffering that our material life can bring. You could say that in a funny literal way *material life stopped mattering.* The union he experienced in his moment of *enlightenment* extinguished every material attachment, unified him with all of Life, and transformed him into a radiant focus of intense insight and attraction.

Released from the perception of impermanence—the cycles of death and rebirth that we all pass through—he attained *nirvana,* and stayed there for the rest of his life, selflessly translating his messages from a blissful alternate reality into this world.

Follow the Directions to a Buddhist Heaven

The path to a Buddhist Heaven lies in the responsibility we each have for the constructive (conscious) or destructive (unconscious) quality of our lives—starting with the understanding that *you are what you think.* Accounting for your life in a constructive way is accomplished through the practice called *mindfulness*—a function of living in the now. Grounding yourself in the moment, focusing exclusively on the task at hand, and avoiding being lost in thought empowers you to liberate yourself from harmful thoughts and actions. Mindfulness creates the freedom accessed by presence.

Discovering Buddhist Heaven is like glimpsing the grounding, luminous nature of spirit (the experience called *bodhi*) that can come only from two essential realizations, the first of which is the *impermanence* of everything. What constantly changes can't possibly satisfy our wishes in a permanent way, so we can't attach our happiness to it, or find the eternal nature of bliss in it. Second, we have to realize that *we actually are the world*—we are made up of the very energies and elements that compose everything in the world, and we have to remain consciously aware of this profound *interdependence* of everything (especially our lives) to everything else—as accumulating, interlocking, cascading energies that constantly create our experience of reality.

The Buddha provides us with a basic list of principles to follow that simplify things in a precise way, composed of the essential rules of life that make up the Four Noble Truths—the way to end suffering he called the Eightfold Path. Here are the Buddha's suggestions for squelching all the pain of life—his path to Heaven:

1. *Right View* or *Understanding,* which means recognizing the impermanence and interconnectedness of all life, so you can see how you realistically fit in. This means you are everything you need—just as you are.

2. *Right Purpose* or *Intention,* which requires aligning yourself and your actions with this proper understanding, and organizing your life around principles that work to end your own suffering and the suffering of others.

These first two steps create the foundation for all the rest. The next three steps describe how to go about your life in a balanced and harmonious way that defuses the force of your ego and reveals your authentic nature, your real personality, and your true purpose:

3. *Right Speech,* which means always telling the truth, never speaking ill of anyone or anything, and speaking with kindness and consideration at all times.

4. *Right Action* or *Conduct,* which means living in a considerate way, respecting all of Life, and selflessly being of service to others.

5. *Right Vocation* or *Livelihood,* which means not earning your living at the expense of others, or at the expense of any life, material security, or well-being of any living beings.

Since our experience of life is based on how we think, the last three steps concern developing a healthy control of what you think about, and what you can accomplish by consciously directing your thoughts:

6. *Right Effort* refers to the effort to control the quality and direction of your thoughts; the vigilance to direct your thinking in harmoniously beneficial ways.

7. *Right Attention* or *Mindfulness* means maintaining the presence to keep yourself aware in the moment, where you can clearly see your options and make proper choices.

8. *Right Meditation,* which is the only real way to train a restless mind, to recognize the delusional thinking that a negative ego would have you believe, and to encourage quality thoughts, inspired by a healthy, positive ego.

The Eightfold Path is a remarkably simple and complete recipe, really, that ends and begins with a basic understanding of how we picture and position ourselves in Life:

We are created by our thoughts; we become what we think. Pain and suffering follow negative thoughts like the wheel follows the ox that pulls it.

We are created by our thoughts; we become what we think. Happiness attaches itself like an inseparable shadow to the positive thoughts that precede it.
—The Dhammapada, 1:1–2

When we choose positive, compassionate thoughts to lead the way, we condition the quality of our life with positive, transformative energy—it really is instinctive. By consciously choosing to direct our thoughts in a good way, we stay connected to the benevolent energy of Life's potential. It's that simple. In directing our thoughts, we create that fully malleable life that doesn't happen *to us,* it happens *for us.*

Using this controlled thinking to detach from chaotic life gives us relief, that's true, but it's only by releasing negativity and then consciously *following it up with focused positive thoughts*—opposing *good* vibrations—that actually empowers us to create the balance and serenity that can shape a better person, and a better world.

Overcome your anger through Love; maliciousness with acts of kindness; greedy desires with generosity; and dishonesty by being honest. Be honest; be kind; be generous—and you'll find happiness.

—The Dhammapada, 17: 221, 223–224

The Buddha's suggestions are so beautifully wise and direct; his path leading to the experience of Heaven is so clear and unclouded. He never describes a place that's anywhere "out there," but a place that exists only *in here*. It just requires loving kindness, right thinking, staying grounded in the unchanging moment, and realizing our profound interconnection with all of life—that's all … and that's everything.

The Gnostic Reunion with Heaven: Ancient Wisdom Lost and Found

Have you ever stood beneath a starry sky looking into the heavens and felt like you were just a visitor here, subject to the beauty and the pain that's the nature of "reality" in this world? Have you felt that there was a distant home of life and light that you'd been exiled from in a way—and that someday you might return there to be reunited with your authentic wholeness and happiness? It's as if the stars were twinkling fragments of that fullness, and you yourself contained a little piece of luminosity, waiting to merge back into a heavenly radiance—then you'd be home, and you'd be free. I've felt that way at times in my life; and in two of my three NDEs, I visited a place like that—a place of luminous Love and light—very much like Heaven.

That feeling I'm talking about—the flash of mysterious understanding that Hindus call *samadhi* and Buddhists call *bodhi*—that glimpse into our familiar spiritual origin is the very essence of *gnosis*. A Greek word meaning "knowledge," gnosis doesn't refer to knowledge in the sense of knowing facts or figures, but instead to the way you know a dear friend or lover—a knowledge that can only come alive in your heart.

The Gnostic ideal, simply put, is that *you really are a displaced part of Heaven,* but during this experience of human life, that knowledge eludes you. Momentarily, you've forgotten your true connection and the way to return, so you've actually come back into this life to rescue your authentic *self,* trapped in your limited perceptions of this world. Within a transformative moment of gnosis, you'll remember who and what you really are, where you really come from, and how to take yourself back home.

In Gnostic mythology, all of humanity is an expression of a divine light imprisoned on an imperfect plane of existence, enfolded in the beauty of earthly existence yet victimized by the suffering that is such a big part of it all. Each of us contains a connecting spark of the Divine Light within called the *pneuma* (what the Hindus might call *atman*). Our fragment, imprisoned in this body, has fallen away from the radiant, infinite matrix of limitless potential, which is our Source called the *pleroma.* Life's sadnesses inspire the longing to reunite our spark with the transcendent unifying power that we inherently know to be our loving origin—the effort to restore ourselves to our authentic nature. When gnosis takes place, we're restored as beings of light. We're liberated and made whole by a "marriage" of all of our opposite aspects—our darkness and light, activity and stillness, desire and contentment, and particularly our masculine and feminine sides. We return to our elemental (even *androgynously)* balanced potential, merged back into the Divine. So gnosis is a kind of a romantic, but nonetheless logical, symbolic journey that can carry us from troubled to transcendent.

While inner discoveries of a spiritual nature may come about through the practice of a chosen religion and the way those practices direct us into the Divine, sometimes they can only occur by rejecting lifelong beliefs that have failed to inspire that peace and sense of belonging-to. Either way, the transformation might require a spiritual rebellion of sorts, and gnosis is all about a mythical subterfuge—an initiation into a secret fellowship that's devoted to returning to Heaven.

Inner Revolution Is Divine Revelation

All great timeless spiritual teachings, like the groundbreaking lessons of the Buddha or the "lost" Gnostic scriptures, are somewhat
revolutionary by definition. All of this timeless, transformative wisdom has the power to shake things up, since an ideological apple cart
or two has to be turned over to force us to consider how to restack
the apples. Revealing the truth is often unsettling. Revelation of the
spiritual world is a revolution in the material one—a rebelliousness,
because after all, you must abandon many of the conventions of *what
society says you are supposed to be* in order to attain an intimate and individual state of fulfillment. You have to be willing to follow a different path, to march to the beat of a different drummer. This divinely
inspired inner rebellion seeks to reunite you with the parts of yourself that have been hidden away, so unlike the deconstruction that
Buddhism elicits, gnosis is a spiritually *restorative* process—the re-
construction of a perfect existing design that's been wrongly defined
by the limitations of material life.

It seems perfect that our exploration into these revolutionary
wisdom teachings comes from a "hidden" text that was literally bur-
ied in time for nearly two thousand years, containing secrets that
were deemed heresy by religious institutions of the day. The Gospel
of Thomas is classified as one of many such Gnostic texts—devoted
to the spiritual transformation and ascension of the spirit by way of
an inward reunion with our Divine Source. In seeking knowledge of
the invisible machinery of Life, the path to Heaven it describes has a
lot in common with our previous two texts in that it requires us to
become spiritual "warriors" and fearless inner explorers.

Directions from East to West
Meet in the Same Place

This beautiful lost and then found scripture also causes us to look
to the East because it presents its ideas in poetic riddles that resemble what Zen Buddhism calls *koans*—quirky, metaphoric aphorisms
posed to provoke the kind of confusion that compels one to break

with conventions and expose underlying realities. Examples of a Zen koan might be *What is the sound of one hand clapping?* or *What did your face look like before you were born?*

Let's discover some of these beautiful, pithy lessons from the Gnostic Gospel of Thomas passed along by a very Eastern teacher, here called *Yeshua*—a sage and poet with the power to unlock our hearts in the eternal *now*, if we supply the proper presence to interpret and engage his directions. And remember, we are always *here* in this presence—wherever *here* is—seeking the inner revolution that can free us.

> Whoever seeks must keep seeking until they find. When they find it, they'll be disturbed; being disturbed they will begin to marvel; then they will rule over All.
> From that moment, they find peace.
> —The Gnostic Gospel of Thomas, logion 2

This describes the actual stages of gnosis: You *need* to look inward, to help get through the painful parts of life; then, when you confront the magical, undeniable interconnectedness of everything, it's disturbingly hard to believe—it sounds a little crazy. But just take a moment and stand back from the world with some spiritual perspective, and you'll realize that a miraculous matrix of luminous people, things, and events is being shown to you in every moment. You'll begin to marvel at what a thoroughly plastic world of experience this is, one that can be experienced deeply and shaped by your attitudes and efforts. Then *you've got it.* You've achieved *gnosis.* You realize blissful peace and happiness are always right *here* and *now.* Then you rule.

Coming to the realization that we live in a miraculous, extra-dimensional reality already is one thing, but how we go about living in our "real" world to make those possibilities come alive is another. When asked his advice about it, our teacher cuts to the chase and asks us to get real about life with straightforward simplicity:

Stop lying. Tell the truth. Don't do anything that goes against
Love. Nothing is hidden in Heaven—everything is exposed.
Everything you've concealed will be revealed; whatever is cov-
ered will be uncovered.
　　—The Gnostic Gospel of Thomas, logion 6

How can we overcome our fears and join up with this Gnostic
revolution of honesty, humility, and compassion? The answer is that
we are already aligned with it; all we need to do is restore these energies of spiritual evolution through the principles we live by and the
actions we take. We need only "covet what we already have" to set
our material minds at ease. Gnosis is the realization that within the
Fullness a great and benevolent resource is always available—despite
the obstacles we place in its way.

Here, this ancient text foreshadows the entire psychological
movement of the twentieth century by giving us some very current
advice on how to eliminate the obstacles we create, the simple means
to reconstruct our sense of wholeness:

When you bring out what is within you, then what is within
you can save you. If you can't bring it out, it will destroy you.
　　—The Gnostic Gospel of Thomas, logion 70

We use the "lost" parts of ourselves to overcome our hardships,
and when we pass through those hardships, we come out on the
other side with more kindness and understanding, empowered by
our humility, directed into more honesty about ourselves, knowing
what forgiveness means to everyone, having compassion for all our
shared struggles, and given the inspiration to contribute to the lives
of others. We become more ready to stick to our path than ever before—and to selflessly help others along the way. We entered into a
"real life"—the Life where we can find Heaven.

Then, when you look out into a starry night, you might be looking right at a planet that's just like Earth, with people and Love and

all of Life's magic—whether you can really see it or not. There's an invisible and subtle essence that's alive in everything on this little spark and in every other twinkle in the night sky.

> I shine the light that shines above Everything. I am the All. All comes from within me, and All comes into me. Split a piece of wood, and I Am within it. Turn over a stone, and you will find me.
> —The Gnostic Gospel of Thomas, logion 77

Within the presence inspired by these ancient texts, we can begin to comprehend the Gnostic *Fullness*, the Hindu *Brahman*, the *impermanence* and *interdependence* that the Buddha teaches. All action and emotion—even matter itself—is entangled in the *now* and can enlighten our path. By restoring our fragment of Divine Radiance back into the light we might call Heaven, we suddenly find we're eternally *home* and eternally *whole*.

The Poetry of Rumi:
Entering the Ecstatic By Way of the Word

So far we've been traveling through kindness, humility, honesty, forgiveness, compassion, and service; through the Bhagavad Gita, the Dhammapada, and the Gnostic Gospel of Thomas into concepts of spiritual perspective and presence, and the most compelling things I've said may have only reached you by this mysterious identification with words on a page, perhaps just a brief turn of phrase evoking deeper understandings that are easier to simply *know* than they are to describe. That's the presence of poetry in whatever choice of words one makes while trying to describe the indescribable.

"Genuine poetry can communicate before it is understood," T. S. Eliot suggested,[14] and when it comes to accessing our unconscious powers of understanding, poetry has always been a foundation of human life existing in music, art, dance, gastronomy, and even architecture, physics, and mathematics—all in the effort to communicate mysteries

---

14. Eliot, *Selected Essays*, 238.

that the material world struggles to recognize and fails to express. Our sense of poetry invites an understanding of powerful intangibles that can only be known through personal experience. It's a lot like trying to describe what Love is like, and in fact, poetry may be the only way to really describe Love, and so to describe Heaven too.

Heaven Is Present in Poetry

The reason for this foray into presence is because there's no better path than poetry, since *poetry is presence*—set down as language. You can't read a poem with your head or your heart anywhere else than right *here* and *now*, can you? You must willingly focus on how poetry speaks within you *now*—or you'll miss the magic. In Gnostic terms, a poem could be considered to be a fragment of that divine fullness—captured like lightning in a bottle. A fragmentary snapshot of a personal heaven you have in "your mind's eye," but the emotionally dimensional landscape that we call Heaven can only be pictured by using our *heart's* eye. Opening that eye is the work of words so well chosen that they transcend the experience of reading—evocations you may not have realized you were missing and longing for, until you read them. Poetry is full of secret doors into an entirely different state of being that can only be called *ecstatic*.

That's the surprise—the sudden cracking open into the radiance, or the coaxing of your surrender into Love that pops and pours through the words of Yeats or Dickinson, Rilke or Neruda, or in this case, the Sufi poet Jalal ad-Din Muhammad Rumi:

> Out beyond ideas of wrongdoing and rightdoing,
> there is a field. I'll meet you there.
> When the soul lies down in that grass,
> the world is too full to talk about
> language, ideas, even the phrase *each other*
> Doesn't make any sense.[15]

---

15. Barks, *Rumi: The Book of Love*, "Soul, Heart, and Body One Morning," 123.

There's something stunningly contemporary about Rumi's poetry, despite the fact that it comes from all the way back in the thirteenth century. He's the world's bestselling, most translated poet, even when his chief purpose clearly seems to be *to tear us apart* with poetry. His aim is to destroy our uncomfortable externals so subtly that we spontaneously dissolve into a kind of bliss. Although you may have never considered this before, it is true—poetry can be so powerful that just the act of reading it can completely alter your energy in a beautiful, balanced way. Read a little Rumi, and after just a couple poems you'll notice that your attitude *will* change. Any existential angst you experience in your body-spirit will start coming into balance with benevolent unseen forces, deconstructing and reassembling your mind and body on a cellular level at the speed at which you read, irrevocably changing you and even the world you inhabit.

Paradise Found in the Clear Desert Air: Rumi's Story

These timeless travels in presence—Rumi's adventures into a poetic Heaven—elicit sensations of a mystical desert journey. The expanse seems clear out to every horizon, populated only by the infinite mind of "the Beloved" in all of its various forms. Human materiality is like window-dressing that dissolves into a shimmering mirage, and the only other important soul to be seen approaching is "the Friend"—a guru or teacher, a brother or sister traveler and seeker of the mystery, a desert *compañero* of the soul. The Friend *is* our soul's completion, sent to rescue us and lead us out of this lovely wasteland, back into the light we deserve to inhabit.

Jalal ad-Din (or Jalaluddin) Muhammad Rumi was born in Afghanistan in 1207 CE and lived in the Turkish town of Konya as a member of a *dervish* learning community, an order of the mystical aspect of Islam called *Sufism*. Coleman Barks, in his book *The Soul of Rumi*, described the goal of the dervishes this way: "The work of the dervish community was to open the heart, to explore the mystery of union, to fiercely search for and try to say truth, and to celebrate the glory and difficulty of being in a human incarnation." [16]

In 1244, Rumi met a wandering dervish ascetic named Shams of Tabriz, and immediately the two men realized that they were *one* in a transpersonal sense—that they were unified with "the Beloved" in one another's presence. For Rumi, *the Friend*—the rescuing half of his own soul—had arrived at last, transforming him forever. When Shams mysteriously disappeared after only four years together, it is said that Rumi, beset by grief, began circling a pole spontaneously, reciting poetry devoted to his lost friend and to the annihilation of his *self* in the pain of separation. That circle became a symbol—acted out in the elegant spinning meditation (called *sama*) that whirling dervishes are famous for.

Sufis consider the heart to be the one true doorway into the Divine, and are devoted to purifying it as a means of realizing the heavenly in any existence. Their four steps to create and maintain that access will probably sound pretty familiar at this point:

1. Freeing oneself from the mental distortions that separate us from our Divine Source.
2. Liberating oneself from the material attractions of life—not *running after the world.*
3. Transcending the illusions created by our selfish ego.
4. Devoting oneself to the complete union with our Divine Source of Being.

As humans, we possess, and are possessed by, an essentially ecstatic spirituality, and it's this heart without boundaries that Rumi's poetry penetrates with such immediacy:

> The clear bead at the center changes everything.
> There are no edges to my loving now. [17]

---

16. Barks, *The Soul of Rumi*, 4.

17. Ibid., "Spiritual Windowshoppers," 53.

With just that simple prompting we can enter into the *ecstatic*—the essential state of feeling like we're in Heaven. All the externals fall away from us like a weight being taken off our shoulders. The boundaries that seem so real from one body to another, from one mind to another, are illusions that we can release—attachments and apparitions that constrain our authentic nature. It's a lot of potential to release with one little stanza.

Words Can Open Worlds within This World

Rumi's house of Love is a joyfully fluid place. You can easily see Heaven from every window, although you might feel guilty that you're not appreciating the view. It's our identification with Life's beauty that lets us forgive ourselves for the little things, and discover our authentic *self* in expressions of transcendence everywhere we look:

> What was said to the rose that made it open
> was said to me here in my chest.
> What was told the cypress that made it strong and straight,
> what was whispered the jasmine so it is what it is,
> whatever made sugarcane sweet, ...
> ... whatever lets the pomegranate flower blush like a human face,
> *that* is being said to me now.
> I blush.
> Whatever put eloquence
> in language, that's happening here.
> The great warehouse doors open; I fill with gratitude,
> chewing a piece of sugarcane,
> in love with the one to whom every *that* belongs! [18]

The loving surrender of our material self (the ego-mind) is not at all a defeat—for Rumi it's the goal, a strategy for returning us to our proper place in the order of the worlds to which we belong. Our

---

18. Barks, *The Soul of Rumi*, "What Was Told," 16.

day-to-day life of ambition and material desire becomes secondary to the strategy of surrender.

> In silence there is eloquence.
> Stop weaving and
> watch how the pattern improves. [19]

Unimaginable joy and power are alive in that humble action, in every moment we realize that we're merely an instrument for expressing Love. So our best designs for life come from following our *karma* with open-hearted kindness, humility, honesty, forgiveness, and compassion, in a spirit of service—with hardly any effort. Then, without the pretense of "'being in charge," everything that carries us shows the way to Heaven.

> The ocean pours through a jar, and you might say
> it swims *inside* the fish!
> This mystery gives peace to your longing,
> and makes the road home home.[20]

How to Find Rumi's Heaven

Rumi suggests that since the Divine consists of *everything,* Heaven can be reliably located only by surrendering into the direction of pain, so we can then turn to find bliss in the opposite direction. Remember— he came to his wisdom by passing through the overwhelming grief caused by the loss of his soul's *Friend,* and while the loss of something we care about never inspires an easy transition, try as we might we can't avoid the bittersweet gift of being transformed by it.

> I saw grief drinking a cup of sorrow
> and called out,
> "It tastes sweet, does it not?"

---

19. Ibid., "The Pattern Improves," 30.
20. Ibid., "The Road Home," 170.

"You have caught me," grief answered,
"And you have ruined my business.
How can I sell sorrow
when you know it's a blessing?"[21]

The poetry of Rumi speaks to us through a language of the heart that can't be communicated in any other way. In an instant, it removes us from the pain of this world and reattaches us to the place that *all* feelings come from. Like the incantations of a spellbinding ritual, his words can all at once liberate our souls, and rejoin them to an unseen world, alive with the energy of Love.

In the presence of the profound wisdom gifted to us through these and countless other teachings from the distant past, we find direction to our own realization of Heaven along paths worn smooth by the footsteps of countless predecessors. Entering into the *eternal moment* alive within these traditions of narrative, life-science, myth, and poetry, we find a reliable road to an inner Paradise—an unchanging "prophet margin" whose bottom line will always lead us to Heaven.

EXERCISE: *Reading Into the Ancient Now*

This is a simple Sunday afternoon exercise that you may have gathered I'd recommend already: simply read at least one of the four selected texts that I draw upon here or any of the many others texts, such as the *Tao Te Ching*, which is always a good choice when seeking timeless wisdom and a proven path to serenity and joy; or the *Lotus Sutra*, the *Chandogya Upanishad*, the *Psalms*, the *Yoga Sutras of Patanjali*, the *Crest Jewel of Discrimination*, *The Sermon on the Mount*, *Pirkei Avot*, the *Hermetica*, *The Enneads*, *Black Elk Speaks*, or a host of other beloved and influential spiritual writings from the distant past. Just pick one that looks good to you, and notice how contemporary its themes actually are—how it speaks directly to you in your heart. Read some Emily Dickinson, or Walt Whitman, or Rumi, or Rabindranath Tagore, and it will surely change your day and, very possibly, your life.

---

21. Ibid., "Twenty Small Graves," 179.

PART III: PURPOSE

*The greatest human quest is to know what one must do
in order to become a human being.*
—Immanuel Kant

In my third Near Death Experience I wasn't given any choice—I was gently forced to come back into this life to fulfill whatever my real purpose was meant to be; yet up to that point, I'd only been successful demonstrating a lot of things I apparently *wasn't* meant to be. What was really required of me was to disassemble what I had thought to be my reality—to recognize most of it as *not being real*— and then to find the underlying authenticity of my life, the divine direction that could lead me out of a clueless darkness and into the light of my true purpose. That means learning to joyfully participate in a world that's much grander and more miraculous than what simply being human normally allows.

It's by reaching an honest, fully enabled view of what's possible in this life (and in the world) that the clarity of divine expression, spiritual evolution, and the revelation of Love can activate the realization of our purpose—to be who we all authentically need to be, and to do what we all authentically agree we must do.

– 10 –
Discovering Divine Purpose
Through Personal Actions:
Becoming a Heavenly Human Being

My first NDE, an out-of-body experience that took me away from my car-crash scene and into a pastoral "heavenly" interview, demonstrated to me that we are spiritual energy occupants riding around in these bodies—a miraculous realization of a limitless new reality—but it didn't quite provide my complete purpose for being in itself.

My second NDE delivered me to a brilliantly illuminated cloud realm where an interactive "screening" of life experiences taught me how important each eternal moment is and will always be. That's a profound piece of insight, but it's still not really an answer to the question *Why am I here?*

But my third NDE was different. It didn't occur in nearly as "heavenly" circumstances as the first two. It was a more elemental, more Earth-bound experience, culminating in being forced back into this world so I could get down to the work that, supposedly, I already knew how to do. In this, my most painful and difficult-to-recover-from NDE, I learned that apparently I did have a special reason for being here—yet none of my hosts on the other side offered up any specifics as to what it was. Somehow I knew I'd have to find that out for myself. After years of struggling with a critical lack of willingness, I was eventually forced into the painful but grateful surrender into Life that led me to an understanding of my own purpose. One reason I came back is to tell you that there are easier ways to do it.

The angels who pushed me back into this world did seem to suggest that *I already knew* deep within myself (or should have known by now) why I'm here and what it is I have to do. While being more to the point may have saved some time, I think their intention was to tell me that the act of getting there really *is the point.* If your authentic self *already* knows why you're here, your real revelations will come from winding your way through life, getting the less authentic parts of yourself out of the way. It's in this process of finding and living your authentic life that your purpose is revealed.

The Ways That Our Purpose Presents Itself

For certain lucky people, discovering *why* they are here is no challenge. Their karma provides them with a clear purpose for how to live their lives right out of the starting gate. The closest I come to that is by starting each day in a bit of a fog, getting to work to clear the fog away, and continuing my daily efforts with all the diligence I can muster. This often serves as a pretty good purpose for being in itself, but being a witness to purer examples can be very inspiring, and all of us can probably think of one or two we've had in our lives.

Many years ago when I was much, much younger, I went on a blind date to a natural history museum with a young woman some friends thought I might like. Although nothing ever came of it, I remember it as having been a lovely day. We wondered over ancient native artifacts and made small talk, finally settling outside on a park bench in the sun when all of a sudden my date did something truly remarkable. She stood up on the park bench, threw her arms out like wings to fly, and loudly announced, "One day I will be a great and famous actor, and everyone will know my name!" People in the park stopped where they were and looked over at this shining girl waving her arms around and smiling, while I, like any young man with a little attitude, was just embarrassed.

The years passed by, and everywhere I went I continued to hear her name as she built a life in the theater, from small repertory companies to larger ones. Finally, years later, she burst onto the silver screen as an "overnight" success, and became a major motion picture star. She was a "great and famous actor" and everyone did know her name—just as she'd proclaimed, standing on a park bench so many years before.

I expect that she had accumulated some perfect karma—a balance in all of her lives up to that point that put her where she simply already knew what she was going to be and exactly how to go about it. Along with providing me with some great inspiration, it made it clear that my life's realization was not so easily known. Like so many of us, I had issues to work through, some karma to balance first, and that would have to serve as my purpose until my efforts could reveal something more.

Along with having to get the bejesus beat out of me to finally become willing to get down to work, I realized that I couldn't just sit and *think* my way out of a purposeless life—that's how it had gotten to be that way. Instead, I had to try harder to *take action* to discover my purpose. I had to live a more conscious, more principled life, to find out what it meant to actually *be* kind, humble, honest, forgiving, and compassionate, and to make myself of service to others, and allow those actions to direct me.

After I tried my new approach for a while, I began to realize that Heaven was never a place for those who fear God but is really available for those who don't experience fear as their prime motivator. The only way for me was through a spiritual approach, designed to disengage my own fearful will and bring me into focus within the bigger picture of Life. From that point on, I began to feel more *wholeness* and to confidently recognize a clearer path ahead.

Maybe Finding Our Purpose Is Simple

Even though the ingredients may be there every day, we don't always wake up knowing what we have to do. Each day may be about opening up to every moment, and proactively engaging the principles that lead us into our potential—not just sitting and trying to figure it out. We discover where we belong by *doing* what we do as well as possible—that's what locates us, and reconnects us to our place in the Universe.

Our participation in this eternal moment connects us to our purpose in the eternal.

I developed an interest in various scripture and old wisdom texts (to my surprise), and as I poured through the material it became clear that all my readings were suggesting the same thing to me— that I'd already been configuring my own place in a part of a greater design. The sages I read pointed toward a restoration of an original connection to Life—a purposeful agreement I may have had from *before I was born*. They opened the door for me to that ethereal, all-knowing realm called *Akasha* (from Sanskrit Hinduism), where the life data—the *Akashic records* of all of our lives through time—is continuously informing our experience of Life. While reading the *Yoga Sutras of Patanjali*, I came across this shockingly simple statement of our purpose: "The universe exists in order that the experiencer may experience it and thus become liberated."[22] Suddenly I saw the basic truth of my purpose: that *Life was living me*—not the other way around.[23] I've always existed to simply express the life I've been given.

I'd been pushed back into this world as a result of every experience I'd ever had, to manifest every capability I'd been given. It was a profound realization of my karma up to that point—all the cause and effect I had been responsible for in my life (or lives). With different karma, I might have been that kid announcing my pure intention, but for me, in this life, it required hardships sufficient to inspire enough humility to be a beginner every day. Then as I read further, every one of those timeless texts proclaimed their own purposes:

The purpose I learned from Hinduism was the recognition of the Divine in everything, the realization of my *atman* (soul) connection to the Divine; and the recognition that selfless dedication of my best efforts to my Higher Power was all that was really required of me. Life was actually easier than I thought.

---

22. Prabhavananda and Isherwood, *How to Know God: The Yoga Aphorisms of Patanjali*, 130. Sutra 2:18.

23. This concept comes from Joseph Campbell, quoted in *Joseph Campbell and the Power of Myth with Bill Moyers*, PBS Television (2001), episode 1, chapter 12.

The purpose I learned from Buddhism was to have absolute respect for all Life, to make an effort to understand myself in a true context that can ease the sufferings we all encounter, and to understand that all Life is indivisibly interdependent, and part of the job is to help all other sentient beings achieve that sense of freedom.

The purpose I learned from the Gnostics was to honor the sanctity of Life, to recognize the eternal in everything, and to complete and restore my authentic (heavenly) spark—my "radiant" Self—to the fullness of being that's alive in Heaven; to realize myself as *an eternal being of light and Love.*

The purpose for living that I learned from Rumi was the selfless dedication to recognizing *the Friend*—realizing the presence of the Beloved in all forms of Life and expression, and the need to *annihilate* my false, material ego-self into the formless, blissful embrace—the unconditional Love—that is the Unknowable Mystery of Life.

To put it plainly, our most basic purpose is simply to escape the ignorance that prevents us from knowing that our authentic divinity is a real, functioning thing, simultaneously shared by every form of Life on this planet.

What We Have to Do Is Who We Are

The reason it can seem that our purpose is eluding us is because we may like to picture it as something rather grand—a life-changing, world-shaking calling or contribution, when in fact it may really be something much simpler. When our ego-minds create those elevated fantasies, our expectations may never be met, and the fear of not living up to some illusion of success can build anxiety and fear. That fear constrains our spiritual imagination and causes us to overlook the powerful truth of all of our lives: *that we are all involved in something very grand already.* We're involved in the miraculous in every moment. Look around you. Open the box you've been sitting on your whole life—your purpose is to be yourself, and to open up to the wonder of it all.

Recently, I met a very intelligent, vibrant young woman who, despite claiming that she lacked the proper credentials, had started her own successful business supplying a needed service to a growing circle of clients. She hadn't felt like she was doing enough, so she and a few associates started hosting a series of talks that turned into an annual conference, bringing together imaginative thinkers and inspirational innovators from all over the country to share their ideas. She was asking me for advice because she felt her life lacked purpose—that she "hadn't found what she was meant to do yet."

The obvious isn't so obvious to us a lot of the time, and she was suffering feelings of inadequacy, even in the face of facts that seemed plain to see—that she was already doing it! The fact is that *feelings aren't facts*, and that much of the time we experience a kind of delusional reality imposed on us by a self-judgmental ego that diminishes the real extent of our contributions to Life.

Years ago, a good friend was in hospice care, dying from an aggressive, malignant cancer. When I went to spend some time with him, I was met at the reception desk by his life partner, who'd been there every day, constantly at his bedside. She was so purposeful, it was almost as if she was in charge of the ward (and in a way she was). The nurses were just his nurses, busy with a number of other people, but *she was his angel*, righteously charged by the intuitive spirit of service, devoted to him as he lay dying.

"My mother died last year," she said quietly to me, "and my brother died the year before." She paused and said, "I didn't know that my life was going to be like this." When I told her that she was answering a remarkable calling, and that her life appeared to be a thing of intensely beautiful service and profound purpose to me, she just looked up through her eyelashes and said, "I *know*," and she smiled a smile that leapt into my heart.

We can all start locating our real purpose by recognizing that *there's nothing here that isn't miraculous.* Our sense of what's "real"—the job title, getting up and going to work, worrying about our finances, isolating ourselves with our countless forms of entertainment—often conceals a deep purpose of Life that's already living through us in plain sight.

If you aren't sure "who you are" at the moment, you may be in a better place than living with the rigid certainty of "this is *it*—this is *who I am*," because that *not knowing* keeps you free to ride your life's changing currents. You're not meant to be one separate, unchanging thing for the whole ride. Instead we are all meant to realize an entire range of mixed blessings through the experiences of our ever-changing lives.

How well we express our true nature adds to (or takes away from) our shared spiritual *evolution*—the opportunity for all of humanity to grow into the expanded Consciousness of Life. We can individually and collectively realize a whole new set of global realities that may presently seem beyond our wildest dreams just by each of us dealing well with the potential of every moment. It's up to all of us to move our great big ball of divine potential toward that Heaven.

These lessons learned are alive in every instant and iota of being...and of course these lessons are really built on one foundation—on the forms of *Love* that manifest themselves through Life, because *Love is the foundation of Life*, and Heaven. Very simply put, *Heaven is Love*, no matter what size or style your life seems to be.

The Natural Purpose of Love

There we finally have it—there is no way around the subject of Love, because how can you go around the essential energy that underlies, surrounds, envelops, and flows into and out of Life in every instant, and whose presence—or absence—gives meaning to all the living experience of the Universe? You can't. And so our purpose, above and beyond anything else, is the expression and evolution of Love as the primary creator of our lives. Our job is to find and recognize Love, and to remove the obstacles that our personal and collective ego-selves have built in between ourselves, Love, and the consciously energized beings we are all designed to embody.

I've got to have things simple, so looking for the Love helps me with my search for purpose in my life; and it's all about being able to see the Love (or lack of it) everywhere I look. The first goal is to enhance our ability to perceive the role Love is playing in the formation of people, places, and things. As you may have suspected, Love provides the entire landscape, the architecture, and the atmosphere of Heaven, and Mother Nature constantly gives me the best examples of this.

Flowers erupt from the ground wherever their seeds happen to get planted for purposes of *expression*—to show themselves off and attract pollinators, leading to the *evolution* of more beautiful flowers. Aside from loving each other, as all living things often do (yes, even flowers have feelings), the flowers turn their lovely faces each day to follow the sun as it crosses the sky. Can you see the Love there, or does it seem unlikely? If you doubt it, the next time you're depressed or anxious, find yourself a park bench in the sun and point your face toward the sun like a flower would and consciously take a few relaxed breaths. After the warmth and light penetrate your spirit for a while, you may start to feel like standing up on that park bench and shouting something positive to the world.

Your Karmic Purpose Is in Every Moment

Each of us is born into very specific circumstances beyond our control, with a particular package of physical traits, talents, and tendencies—all of which are transient characteristics that can be molded and developed to form who we become, materially speaking. That's the action of karma. None of it guarantees happiness, or the sense of fulfilling a true purpose in Life, but there's something in every life that does: the discovery of our spiritual reality. It's our avenue to finding purpose and (like Love itself) the medium in which all of our plastic potential can find its utmost expression…which may mean movie stardom or making beds in a spiritual retreat. Our job is to follow Divine Guidance as well as we possibly can to make the most of what we've been given—not only the personal package of quantum, karmic "data" that makes us "this or that," but the greater responsibility of stewardship that our form gives us in this world.

Our karma is a framework we can use to work within and to realize our true purpose. Like an identifying bracket, it locates us within the infinite field of Creation when we fully release our will to control things, so we have to start with the strategy of surrender that allows us to really *use* it. Then we can operate at the deep level where Creation is indivisible—and that's where the blind faith we need comes from. We can *trust* this invisible structure—even though it can be difficult to see it at work—because the real results of spiritual solutions aren't easy to imagine looking ahead; however, they always become gorgeously obvious when we look back at our lives.

Choosing to be entirely honest, doing the right thing, showing up in your unique way with no regard for your own gain, causing no injury, and recognizing and following Love in your life—these decisions will prove to be the best things you've ever done, in retrospect. When you can be proactive with these spiritual tools—carry them right out front—you guarantee the best outcomes for all. It will develop your faith in who you are meant to be, and confidence in what you can accomplish.

When you're not sure of yourself, ask yourself this: What do the spiritual partners in your life *want* you to do? What do they *need* you to do? Once you recognize the indivisibility of the Divine, those directions—filtered by Love—are the keys to forming your karma. If you are a fabulous piano player right out of the gate, play the piano! If your favorite aunt is sick and needs help, get right over there and show up for her. If the benefit picnic asks you to make potato salad for fifty, make a big batch of the best potato salad they've ever eaten. Don't even question these obvious, Love-inspired directions. There's a simple set of priorities you can follow: What does the Universe give you to do? What can you do to help your life partners the most? And last (but not least) of all, what do you want for your own life? Answering the first two will answer the third.

Divine Consciousness always seeks your union with others and with Life. People want your unconditional love and support. The world needs your particular talents and creative expression. Life needs you to be a responsible, caring, involved participant! When you embrace this lovely reality, finding your purpose is easily alive in every moment.

EXERCISE: *Finding Your Purpose Finder*

When you're wondering what your purpose in life is, just grab a piece of paper and a pencil, pull up a chair, and get ready to make a couple lists. First, list all the things you loved to do when you were a kid. In a column alongside that, list the things that you were expected to do or that people wanted you to do: go to school, take care of your little sister, do yardwork, draw pictures, play music, participate in sports, take care of pets or animals, perform, make things, etc. Now notice where the two lists converge.

Next, make an adult version of the same list. First, list all the things you love to do, everything that really interests you, and what your wishes for the future might be. Include the people you love as entries on this list. Then list everything you're expected to do—your work and responsibilities, what people *want* you to do and rely on you for, and your ideal goals for the future. Add to this list the people who need your help or whom you're responsible for. Also add the important, serious life events that you've shown up for, or intend to show up for, the best way you can. Notice where the two lists converge again.

After making these lists, reread them, open your heart, and intuitively you'll receive empowerment for your true purpose at the level of your authentic self.

– 11 –

Looking into the Truth:

Turning from Our Dark Corners to Face the Light

It's hard to see through the complicated surface of life sometimes, isn't it? We may try to hold on to our spiritual view, but it's a difficult connection to maintain. In certain transcendent moments, spirituality seems practically self-activating, but when you're dealing with the trials of everyday life, it can be a different story. My experiences demonstrated to me absolutely that we're energetic, spiritual beings, but here we occupy *this* human form that unavoidably defines our experience of Life. It can be humbling to look at the sensory capacity of other creatures and realize how limited our powers of perception really are. Creatures in nature live in a richer world of sounds and smells, where some can actually see in this dark—without the kind of complicated processing that's always entering our human minds.

We can go back to the evolution of the human brain throughout millennia and blame our disconnection on the *amygdala*—the ancient part of the brain that apparently incites so many of our instinctive fears. Since fear often seems to be the language of our ego, it might help us to consider that some of that noise may just be leftover survival impulses—vestiges of a prehistoric stage of spiritual evolution. Gaining some awareness of these ancient tendencies is part of the process of finding happiness and security, since the only saber-toothed tigers left to fear are the ones that live in between our ears.

The way we look at life is how we see it. When we identify with our ego-mind, we get caught up in unnecessary fears, and can look right past the potential of our lives. What can make it really tough is when we become so accustomed to our illusions that we mistake them for reality.

The expression "to lighten up" is an important suggestion to anyone suffering from the material negativity that always tells us both that our life is heavier and has more *gravity* than it actually has, and that things are always *darker* than they seem. Look around without the "glass darkly," and you can't help but notice that life is actually lots of fun, sometimes very funny, and occasionally downright hilarious. Gloomy situations can often be easily exposed as frauds—bad efforts to hide a good time that can be revealed and healed by shining some kindness on them and inviting in a little shared, silly camaraderie.

Unfortunately, there are a few things that humans tend to do that feed those material delusions—unconscious impairments of our spiritual vision that seem difficult to avoid. They're usually subtle "natural" flaws that are hard for us to perceive in ourselves but that really stand out in any coffee klatch in Heaven (and yes, they do have really good coffee there).

How Biased Perspectives Distort Our Vision

Some of our most common obstructions come in the different forms of *biases* that we might engage in unconsciously. A common example of this would be assuming that leaders are *men,* not *women.* It's unconscious selective thinking that's a little like playing a dumb version of God without realizing it. Let me go through these four wrong ways we tend to look at life.

The first one is the "in-group/out-group bias," which makes us think we belong with people who *look* like us, and that we share a set of fundamental qualities with those who appear to be "like us." Actually, every human shares the same fundamental qualities—whether we look the same or not. (We all look the same from *on high*—which naturally is a very diverse place.) Falling prey to this bias makes it hard to experience wholeness, living in a state of closed-off judgment and comparison. As Dr. Wayne Dyer always said, "When you judge others, you don't define them, you define yourself."[24]

Our second case, "affinity bias," is when just because someone has experiences like yours, you think you should have a lot *more* in common with them—like if you're from the same town or went to the same school. Misery doesn't love company, it really loves more misery, and materially based identifications are stewpots of destructive beliefs and attitudes. We do have a lot in common with one another, but keep in mind that we may be on a different part of the cosmic learning curve, so just because we're fellow alumni doesn't mean that our new acquaintance knows the way to our spiritual reunion.

Next up is "anchor bias," which is when you relate an assumption or conclusion about one experience (or thing or person) to *all the rest of the same*. For example, "My teenage daughter scratched the car, so all teenage girls are bad drivers," or "I once saw a bald guy throw away perfectly good yogurt, therefore all bald guys waste yogurt." You can see how those silly blanket assumptions could lead to some damaging misconceptions—especially when we're not aware of them.

The last of these is my favorite, I'm afraid, because of all the times I've suffered from unconsciously perpetrating it myself. It's called "confirmation" bias, and it boils down to *always wanting to be right*. The result is that anything that challenges a preconceived belief is summarily rejected—even if there's plenty of evidence for it being true. If it disturbs the ego's set worldview, it's out—and likely to be vilified later. As a consequence, you seek out only what confirms your beliefs, warranted or not. There's a lot of this these days, with the media (and social media) compartmentalization of our worldviews—it fragments our humanity, based on all of these biases. A persistent problem for me is that my confirmation bias can prevent me from fairly examining understandably different ways to look at the same issue.

---

24. Dyer, *Everyday Wisdom*, 152.

Biases are easy to spot once you know what they are—they're almost always some form of unconscious self-importance. It's always I am *this* or I am *that*, when the truth is that I am really only those things *in my own mind*, while in the greater Divine Mind that we're all a part of, we're all much, much more.

A Simple Trick of Grammar
Can Help You Find the Truth

I really just want to have a simple, hooked-up, plugged-in knowledge of what I am: a beautifully fragile, flawed, creative, and potentially loving expression of Divine Source, along with my wife, my kids, my occupation, a nice meal on the table, and a little sunshine on my face...But it's just not going to happen that way all of the time. I need some tools to help lift me over the self-created obstacles that block my spiritual view, especially when I *like* those obstacles. I need ways to trick my ego into leaving the room, so I can lock the door behind me and be happy in a room full of transcendent connectedness—a room with a view of Heaven.

In this human form, I find that material life is like a vacuum—especially since it comes with so many attachments. It's easy to get sucked into all of the common biases, day-to-day definitions, and material demands of my life. While I can forget my divine connections in *an instant*, it seems that any time I'm not truly present, I can instantly become obsessed with all the material things that "I am supposed to be." I can quickly forget my own Divine Source.

All of the temporary aspects of my life—the *externals*—have always been changing, even when I don't want them to; and it's the instinctive, unconscious effort to control these changing parts of life that sucks us in, isn't it? One of the best spiritual tools I've ever come across is a simple language trick that helps me distinguish what parts of my life are always changing from what parts aren't. It may be obvious to you that grammar isn't my strong suit, but even an amateur analysis of sentence structure can help open the window in my heart up to a superior view of the Divine.

Ramana Maharshi, a wonderful twentieth-century Indian swami, put his finger right on an important point of fact when he simply said (and I paraphrase), "The only important part of 'I am this, or I am that' is the 'I Am' part."[25] It is always the second half—the "this or that" part, that is the problem." With that helpful grammatical foot up from the good swami, we can see the distinction between the start of those statements we make about ourselves, "I am," and the finish, *"this or that,"* and how easy it is to separate spirit from the material:

"I am bored; I am an American; I am still waiting to get paid for that job; I am victimized by my landlord; I am smarter than all of those people; I am detaching from that; I am very spiritual."

What changes and what doesn't change in all of those statements? You'll notice the second part, the *"this or that,"* is what changes, or can always change. It's the movable part. The first part, the subject, "I am," always stays the same. So if we simply drop the second part, the first part is our connection to the eternal Self—the part that we all share! In this easy, open-ended way, we're directed straight into the mystery, the common ground that we all spring from and stand upon. It's how *we are all the same.* That little *I am* can compassionately connect us to each other, and to all of Nature, all the plants and animals, the oceans and the Earth—even to the stars and the Universe itself. It's a pretty big trick for such a little bit of grammar. *I Am.*

Then it's hard not to notice how that second part grammatically *separates* us from the Divine, by opening the door to our painful regrets, fantasies, expectations, and sense of self-entitlement:

"I was once the Homecoming Queen; I was really the first person to use that technique; I am more deserving of that promotion than anyone else; I am going to lose weight." I am quite sure that none of that really matters.

Just catching ourselves and stopping at "I am" immediately reconnects us to the real substance of Life, and appropriately *disconnects*

---

25. Natarajan, *A Practical Guide to Know Yourself,* 41.

us from the unnecessary desires, fears, conceits, and the like—our troublesome attachments to the vacuum of the material.

Honest Self-Examination Can Uncover Your Spirit

Self-centeredness tends to be unavoidable, living in our own skin as we do. Unfortunately, selfish preoccupations are the cause of the worst karma and the most stubborn impediments along our path. Naturally, everyone is embroiled in their own story of themselves. If your self-story is anything like mine, it's mildly heroic (in what I would hope to be an appropriately humble way). I try to think about myself positively, and so I've consciously (and even subconsciously) fashioned a fairly favorable version of my own personal history, one that's full of challenges, disappointments and victories, and ups and downs, with a happy ending—like a good movie.

One thing is certain: I have a lot at stake in this carefully crafted picture of myself, and when my story is challenged by some inconvenient fact, I tend to automatically write those parts out to avoid "pain." This characteristic (similar to the confirmation bias that I mentioned earlier) is called *cognitive dissonance,* and it becomes a lot like confidently driving in the dark without your lights on. Disassociating from reality to spare our ego and spite ourselves seems to be a modern twist on an ancient survival instinct—a wayward wish to somehow protect ourselves.

Fortunately, we're actually part of a forgiving Divine Consciousness, and the tools we've learned to keep us in the fold—kindness, humility, honesty, compassion, service, etc., can save the day when we're being driven into the darkness by blind ego. We just need the awareness to activate them. And for that express purpose, we experience dis-ease. We experience *pain.* In that uncomfortable way, pain is a gift—and even though it hurts me to say it, *pain is usually a wake-up call.*

For years, it never occurred to me that the areas where I wasn't being entirely honest in my own story were the same areas where I seemed to experience pain in my life. It was like I'd handcrafted some protective finish to conceal a blemish in the smoothed-out story of *who I am*. Some part of me always needed to be right, so it secretly suppressed the shameful knowledge that I wasn't *always right*—that I wasn't being entirely honest—until finally something (bad) had to happen to open my eyes to the uncomfortable truths hidden in my story.

This is where the stuff we usually avoid becomes just the stuff we really need. In the course of an honest self-examination, my growing discomfort made me realize that there was somebody at work inside of me, functioning as an anonymous, invisible editor, designing my story and obscuring my uncomfortable truths. My shadow editor was going about his business, quietly covering over the source of my white lies, my misjudgments, my lack of self-forgiveness, my fears of failure. If he didn't do his job, I might be discovered to be a fraud, and lose something I couldn't afford to lose, or fail to get something that I "needed to have"—imaginary fears left over from some ancient instinct. It was like *me and my shadow strollin' down the avenue,* as the old song goes.

So while it may sound crazy to call attention to our discomforts, it may be literally more crazy *not to,* since it's probably the best way to reveal the blemished reality of our self—our actual pathology, as it were. Since our pathology isn't really a choice but more like an inner geography, those patterns of denial aren't something to avoid, but are something to explore.

A Little Suffering Reveals the Truth

What if our discomforts and dis-eases exist to force us to look beneath our fragile human surface and discover the true source of human pathology at work—to throw open the spiritual windows of our heart and shine a little divine light on it? What if following the light that comes through the broke-open crack could lead us to the end of our self-imposed exile from Heaven? The attention paid to our pain would be well worth that trip out of the darkness, don't you think?

In this light, even the attraction of simple sadness is seen as a divine mechanism to open our hearts and give us a better view of who we really are.

With my eyes and my heart opened up this way, I can finally, naturally, escape the self-centered importance of *my* story and begin to help others write a more successful story for all of us. Perhaps my pain can free me to help ease someone else's pain, and help them to realize that we're all writing in the same book. Now the story really starts getting brighter for everyone, as selfishness is replaced by *selflessness* and the desire to control is replaced by the desire to be of service.

In Buddhism, this effort toward mutual illumination is called *bodhicitta*, and serious Buddhist monks can almost go a little overboard on this path to self-realization and transcendence. Listen to the idealism in this enthusiastic embrace of pain by the guru Lord Serlingpa: "Adverse conditions are spiritual friends. Devils and demons are emanations of the victorious ones. Illness is the broom for evil and obscurations. Suffering is the dance of what is." [26]

Suffering is the dance of what is. Wowee! The painful exile we tend to impose on ourselves usually comes from the desire to control things, and the truth is we really can't, can we? So our surrender into the mystery of Life becomes a very effective strategy for peace and happiness. To find our true purpose in the eternal, we transcend the human form but we don't abandon it—we move our spirits through it, like a benevolent passer-by, and experience the unique opportunities that only this form can provide for us to learn our eternal lessons.

Love Shines Its Light on the Path to Authenticity and Truth

I'd like to return to Love—and suggest that once our eyes and hearts are open, it's really the only way to keep them open, and avoid the darkness for good. I propose that the energetic inspiration of every form of Life we perceive with our eyes (and our hearts) comes out of the *field* of Love—the Source of Divine Illumination.

---

26. Kongtrul, *The Great Path of Awakening*, 45.

Like the light reflected in the faces of wildflowers growing through the cracks in the blacktop, forms that are natural, efficient, and beneficial emanate the light of Love and are easily discerned from forms that are forced, wasteful, and destructive—forms that come from a lack of Love. The shapes, ingredients, intention demonstrated, feelings evoked, and senses excited by these forms tell the whole story, so if you're looking at Life the right way, *you can see the Love in everything* (as well as where you may need to provide it).

We all know Love is easy to see in Nature; in fact, you really can't escape it—but witnessing it at work in the "man-made" material world isn't quite so easy. Let's have a look at the Love in the forms of art, architecture, and food (and then later, each other) for the purpose of becoming more conscious of the actual energetic, illuminative power of Love.

From the earliest cave paintings of Lascaux to the perfectly scribbled abstract expressionism of any five-year-old, art has always been a vehicle for the energy of Love. It's nearly as obvious there as it is in Nature—in fact, it's an expression of the authentic nature of humans. Passion drives the pen, the brush, and the body; channels open up to the mystery, and our hearts open up to a longing and connection that can't be communicated in any other way. Since art is the language of the soul, and Love is the language of the soul, they are both speaking the same language of the heart. Witness the Love arising and emanating from all forms of artistic expression, and the sense of timeless presence that the appreciation of art evokes. Art is the poetry of Love in action.

The forms of our homes, habitats, and gathering places have always been a direct indication of our heart's intent too—the amount of Love that's expressed in their making. We need shelter, and inviting, comfortable shelter is best—so it's part of our spontaneous creative nature to build it with Love. When our eyes are open just right, it becomes evident in the forms and materials that are used just how much Love has played a part in their construction—the qualities, aesthetics, and caring intentions, and to what degree they benefit our world and fit the architectural scheme of Heaven.

Some buildings are cheap and unattractive. Some radiate intimidation or entitlement, but others offer thoughtful qualities for people to live with and share in. These could be the rooms in the mansion of the human heart—hosting the spiritual energies and exchanges of Love. Seek those places out, and absorb the energy alive in their shapes, spaces, windows, and walls. Should you build a building, build it with Love, and the sense of responsibility that it engenders.

Food is a no-brainer. Everyone knows that Love is the major ingredient in all the tastiest, healthiest food. The forms of Love-food are pretty obvious, because they stick close to Nature. There's always Love in simple, fresh, carefully prepared ingredients, arranged and presented with artistry and spirit—you can see it, you can smell it, and best of all, you can *taste* it. It's easy to realize that food supplies that energy to you. You are what you eat, so where you see the Love in food, *eat that*—because it connects you to Spirit, it's your soul's true sustenance. That's what's on the menu in Heaven.

Last but not least, let's look at people. Once again, with what the Hindu call *sakshi*, the non-judgmental witnessing of life, we can *see* how much Love has gone into the formation of a person from their bearing, expressions, and attitudes. The obstructions to Love that exist in their psyches are reflected in their exterior physical and psychological expressions, as well as in their sometimes destructive, disconnected goals and the results of their actions. It's no coincidence that the quantity of Love expressed mirrors the level of Consciousness realized. That's the spiritual evolution for which Love is the Source.

Witnessing the radiance of Love issuing out of the forms around us is critical, because at those moments that you're seeking help, the Universe is constantly showing you the path to follow. Follow the outward forms of Love in your choices—where you live and go, what you eat and wear, the art and entertainment you take in, how you vote, the company you keep, and how you behave—and you won't need to worry about anything else. Simplify your life around this comforting ethos. Follow what feels right *in your heart*, and everything else will come from following that intuitive direction. Where there is a lack of Love in the forms around you, supply it yourself or, if possible, get help supplying it. With these methods, we stay connected by the matrix of Love to our authentic selves and our true purpose to serve one another and our planet.

We start to see directly past the surface of things and people— even through the veil of sadness that is the illusion of Life—to the light within. Ah, *sadness*. Sadness is like spiritual x-ray vision in this life. It activates our ability to see the Love in all of the changing forms around us. It activates kindness, and humility, and honesty, and forgiveness, and compassion, and allows us to remain joyfully engaged in our spiritual life, regardless of how rough it seems sometimes.

Remembering our authentic purpose begins with holding our spiritual essence in one hand, and the physical world of matter in the other, and then recognizing the Love that binds them together as an expression of Divine Consciousness. In order to see the world in its true light, simply ask yourself this: *Does what I see come from Love, or is it from Not-Love?* The greatest power of Love isn't the power of being *in love*, it's the power of Love *in being*.

Remain Open to the Miraculous

Living in your spiritual conscious awareness, you can't help but notice that much of the world is trapped in a kind of collective *cognitive dissonance*. A lot of people live in a blindness of denial that insists there's only the single surface reality at play in this life. This collective blindness insists that nothing is miraculous, when, in fact, everything is. Keep your eyes open to Love—*don't go back to sleep*. Sometimes the truth is hard to recognize through this veil of human illusion.

It can be a lot of fun to expand our experience of the miraculous by embracing what is sometimes referred to as the "paranormal," from the Greek *para*, meaning "to run alongside of, or beyond," which suggests the extra-dimension of Spirit. A round Earth was once considered paranormal but literally expressed a different dimension than the best minds of the day could allow. Many esteemed past and present members of the Flat Earth Society have wholeheartedly believed in Heaven, but have failed to realize that Heaven is essentially a paranormal concept too.

The embrace of paranormality is just a willingness to keep our eyes wide open to new realities—the possibility of opening and creating extra-dimensional worlds—like making *Heaven on Earth* a new reality. It exposes the potential for discoveries in fields like the generation of free and limitless power, suppressed archeology, remote viewing, "non-local" (or spiritual) communication, the search for life beyond Earth, and much more that may be considered a little crazy now but will look quite sane in the not-too-distant future.

I know that my experiences of the afterlife were definitely extra-dimensional, and that Heaven is the experience of an extra-dimensional state of being. The three times I checked out, my body stayed here, but my spirit continued into an entirely different realm—a non-physical realm created by pure Consciousness. Much of what used to be called science fiction is now simply called *science*, and slowly but surely science is completely reassessing what Consciousness is, and the role it plays in a more complete theory of a synchronistic, multi-dimensional Universe.

As we learn to look beyond the darkness that can be such a big part of our human experience, we discover all the best ways of opening our eyes to the light of the Divine.

EXERCISE: *Teach Your Eyes to Look for Love*

The next time you have a day free to yourself, leave your home with a different intention than usual, and go out into the world intent on looking for the Love and light in everything you see. Put all judgment and comparison on hold, and just observe Life. Are some forms disagreeable or aggravating? Are some gently attractive? Do things look "good" or "bad" to you, and why? How does the light affect the surfaces and colors of what you look at? Is the weather changing the day around you? Do some people seem to carry painful body language, while others project light and energy? Observe a child's play, the life of a tree, the activity at a bus stop, the amount of love in your lunch. Behold every moment as though you were witnessing *a miraculous expression of energy*.

- 12 -
Meditation Works
When Your Mind Doesn't:
Don't Just Do Something—Sit There!

The gift of clarity and comprehension that meditation energizes in us is a true phenomenon of human potential, but encouraging people to sit around and do nothing can sound like a real curiosity. In my experience, people who haven't experienced meditation for themselves are really surprised by how life-changing it can be. I understand. I mean, how can sitting around doing nothing actually change anything?

In fact, meditation changes *everything*, because it functions for us in profoundly practical ways: by fortifying our emotional stability, intellectual understanding, and physical wellness; and, as the catalyst of our spiritual potential, by awakening transpersonal powers of intuition and sensory expansion. Without sounding too otherworldly, I'd like to testify that meditation *is* otherworldly—the opening within ourselves to an extra-sensory dimension, a realm of Love and positive perception that we could call Heaven.

NDE survivors will tell you that there's something very different about "the other side," and that was true for me all three times. The experiences of my *self* and my reality were completely different from anything I'd ever known before. It wasn't like a dream—not as disconnected or random. I felt very, very *alive*, in an indescribably kind of effervescent way. I experienced no sense of anxiety at all and felt absolute peace and ease. I wasn't attached to my thought process, as in normal life, but *connected* in a way I'd never felt before, as though

I'd been integrated into a grounded, expansive mind that was *every-where*—an intelligence that I wasn't generating but was *contained by*. Those three sensations of intensely conscious awareness (aliveness, ease-of-being, and connectedness) that I experienced while I was totally "unconscious," are feelings that I never consciously experienced again—until I began meditating.

I can understand how someone might think that sitting in meditation would be a terribly boring thing to do. Trying to think about *not thinking* sounds a little pointless. The first things that came to my mind when I first tried to meditate were mostly default feelings of resistance; I just really didn't want to sit there "doing nothing." Now I can't imagine Life without it. I've discovered that meditation can—and will—open an *interdimensional channel* within me by just sitting in one place. That's a pretty life-changing thing to have happen for you while sitting around "doing nothing." If you don't believe it, give it a try, and it will literally *change your mind*.

Going Way Beyond by Just Sitting Around

I need to be able to practice without a lot of fuss, so I've developed a way to meditate that I can do almost anywhere, pretty much any-time. And the miracle of it is that I can experience those sensations of aliveness, ease-of-being, and connectedness whenever and wher-ever I give myself the space to sit for a while. When I first began meditating, I was trying to use it to get through a hard time, but I was trying too hard. In my ignorance and impatience I was looking for instant magic, a quick fix. I did everything you're supposed to do to get ready, and then I'd sit there and think, *All right, I'm meditat-ing…I'm sitting here, and I'm meditating.* That would go on for about ten minutes until I would throw in the towel and turn on the TV. Something like that may happen automatically for a lot of us, so let's take a minute to think about what to think about when you're not supposed to be thinking.

At first when we sit and *try not to think* we tend to fail, because we're so accustomed to identifying our life with our thought process.

Try to *not* think, and stuff pops up, particularly like *I've only got a half an hour for this*. Then, as you sit longer more random, semi-crazy stuff comes up, like *I've got to call that guy back ... When will the landlord fix the front door? Is an asteroid going to hit the Earth? What am I going to eat for breakfast?*

All these different unrelated thoughts occur in a *serial* fashion— that is, one leads haphazardly to the next and to the next, sometimes connected by the barest thread that only makes sense right at the moment it connects. A few more turns of the wheel down that road, and you can't even remember how you got there, or why, because there is no why—that's just how our mental processes work when we're not paying attention. Our typical thought process is created by the incessantly demanding nature of our thinking organ, our brain, which like some kind of wild, prehistoric shark, instinctively insists on constant movement—and it's that restless, relentless movement that leads us to what the Buddha warned of when he said (and I paraphrase): "We are created by our thoughts; we become what we think. Pain and suffering follow negative thoughts like the wheel follows the ox that pulls it." One minute we're fine, and the next we're stuck in an uncomfortable place.

An important lesson of meditation that you may have never considered is this: *Thought requires Consciousness, but Consciousness does not require thought.* Descartes was a little off when he said "I think, therefore I am," because we *are* whether we're thinking or not—and all of us have experienced that liberating feeling we get when we "didn't have a thought in our head." Practicing meditation can make that feeling a regular option, not just a fleeting moment of mental freedom.

Our problems occur when thoughts become unintentionally painful and begin to cascade down into places we really don't want them to go. Our ancient ego becomes uncontrollably reactive, and we can suddenly think our way straight into a little hell of our own making. Yet with just a little practice, most of us can stop that process by being *mindful*—the simplest form of that discipline being the common self-request *I don't even want to think about it anymore,* and then we don't think about it.

Meditation helps us formalize that discipline and gives us the option to exert more control over our thinking process; that's all…but that's a lot. Imagine being able to witness more of the sanity, clarity, and beauty of Life as a regular product of a healthy thought process, instead of being subject to wayward negativity. Imagine being able to encourage more relaxed *conscious awareness* all the time.

When we sit in meditation, we're really trying to witness and objectify this serial inner monologue and to try to wear it down until it begins to submit, or to side-step it completely, like a bull-fighter (or more literally like a bull-*avoider*).

That sideways simile describes what our very appropriately named *right brain* is doing while our *left brain* is acting as a serial processor, calculating, organizing, and arranging things. The right hemisphere of our brain functions concurrently as a kind of *parallel* processor, connecting our sensory experiences holistically (engaging "non-ordinary" perception), which leads to a much easier and more appreciative experience of Life. Your right brain is in play when you experience beauty, art, creativity, melody, sadness, serenity, happiness, and all of those wonderful, intangible, "unrealistic" joys of Life. It engages whenever you're looking for, and hopefully finding, emotional resonance and Love.

Unfortunately, our right brain gets short shrift because of the sequentially demanding nature of contemporary life: *Go there! Do this! Do that!* Our ego can manifest its own kind of *cognitive dissonance,* ignoring the holistic data enjoyed in our right brain because it doesn't support a "realistic"-enough worldview—it has nothing to do with the demanding inventories and elaborate justifications that your "realistic" ego insists on. "Get real!" people exclaim, which usually actually means "Get negative!"

When we start being able to sit longer in meditation, we can consciously engage that holistic experience and hold ourselves in a balanced state where we discover that most demanding thoughts aren't really so important. Life can be experienced in a *more* realistic way when we are in this way "less realistic," because we recognize that the actual moment we're living in is fine *as it is*. Life isn't really full of sequential demands or threatening "realities" at all—those are mostly imaginary delusions thrown up by our prehistoric ego. Equipped with the conscious awareness that a meditation practice gives us, we can start freeing ourselves from unnecessarily demanding thoughts. Nothing really *needs* to happen right at this moment—unless a bear is heading your way or you're sitting on something wet.

The escape from serial thinking delivers us into *presence,* and the power and comfort alive in the eternal moment. It's a presence for Life that's only possible when we can gain some control on the courses we run through our heads, and meditation allows us an easy awareness of those different parts of inner life—the duality of material ego versus our extra-dimensional spirit. When we can identify ourselves with our loving, spiritual nature, we become more effective in our demanding daily lives, because the *ease* in our thinking makes it easier to gets things done.

As we sit making space in our thoughts, we experience a sense of joyful transcendence and a sense of unity that's impossible to experience when we're pent-up and weighed-down by material demands. There's the presence of that graceful intuitive intelligence, rising up through our more spacious thinking, informing our decision-making and problem-solving with fresh clarity and confidence.

Getting our mind to become accustomed to that sounds good, doesn't it? But how do we get there? Let's go *into* it and talk about a few ways to make it work, starting with what our goals for a meditation practice can be—the threefold advantages we might gain by incorporating meditation into our schedule:

1. To develop a deeper sense of presence and an immediate sensation of Life in the eternal moment.
2. To become a witness to our thoughts and gain control over the quality and direction of our thought process, separating our true self from our delusional ego.

3. To unite our authentic inner self with all divine Being, Love, and Life in the Universe.

Nice goals, right? As a means to practice, you'll hear the concept of "single-pointed concentration" referred to in meditation instructions, and I think it's a concept that's best illustrated by graphic similes like these three very useful images:

• Your mind is like a candle that can be upset by a breeze; you need to steady that candle like a still, golden flame in the dark.
• Your mind is like the smooth surface of a pond, and wayward thoughts are like ripples that need to be smoothed out.
• Your mind is like a mirror reflecting Consciousness; when unwanted thoughts appear as smudges and streaks, you need to keep wiping the mirror clean.

As you make an effort to meditate, here's a little truth you might consider about the unique mental capacity and potential of human beings: *We are actually designed to do this,* and much more. We possess an evolutionary "transpersonal" spiritual sensory function that we are meant to develop—and meditation is the best way to do it.

The Place and the Position

You can find some great how-tos on meditation from online advisors to the ancient masters. Any well-intended self-help resource will have a lot of good suggestions. The Bhagavad Gita devotes the entire sixth chapter to meditation, including how to sit and what to sit on (although deerskins aren't really a household item these days); and chapter 3 of the Dhammapada, entitled "Thought," is all about it too. Joining group meditations can be great if practicing with others sounds good to you.

My basic approach to meditation is simple. Find a clean, warm-enough, quiet-enough place. Be comfortable, but not too comfortable; our goal is single-pointed concentration and relaxed unity, not sleep. Sitting in a chair is a good practice for meditating on a train, plane, or bus, but making like a real swami by sitting cross-legged in half-lotus position (if possible) is what I find to work best. Don't get in a spot where any kind of pain preoccupies you, so sit on a cushion or a folded blanket. I like to sit on a slight slope, where your feet naturally rest a bit lower than your tailbone. Then imagine a "golden string" pulling straight up your spine, attached to the crown of your head (with one of your angels gently pulling it straight up toward Heaven). Take a couple deep breaths, and when you exhale, relax your neck and let your shoulders hang from your spine like a balanced mechanical rack. Keep your chin line parallel to the ground. And that's it—you're ready to go.

I always like to sit in peaceful nature, if possible, but if not, you can burn sage or mild incense and play recorded nature sounds, *Oms,* healing *ragas,* Reiki session soundtracks, or hemispheric-balancing recordings; all are favorites of mine, especially as long as they're not too melodically involved. Vocal guided meditations can be very helpful, but are different from this simple effort, which is: *How do I just sit alone and make the "magic" happen?*

The problem starts when we sit down to clear our mind, and it just doesn't want to clear by itself. It's hard to turn off our thoughts and go straight into that calm *nirvana* that meditation will lead us into if we practice, practice, practice, so we have to find ways to control our thought processes more objectively and intentionally.

Here are three approaches to dealing with the challenge of a noisy mind, culled from my experience. What we hope to resolve is this: *What do we think about when we want to learn to control our thinking, and how can that lead us to a serene and focused place? Or, how can we get to Heaven by just sitting here?*

1) Analytical Meditation

Since thinking is a process that demands movement, let's start by objectively recognizing all of that movement and putting it to good use.

In what I call *analytical meditation*, the object is to observe our thoughts. You might begin by saying to yourself *I'm going to sit and quietly think about my thinking*, and then *become a witness* to the predominant thoughts forming on the internal stage of your mind. How do they connect to each other, and where do they lead you? Do certain thoughts inspire certain feelings, and invariably inspire more thoughts and feelings in the same direction? Does the process demand that you make an entire, often familiar loop through a whole set of strung-together thoughts, leading you back to some unresolved state where you begin that loop all over again?

As was the case when I first started, we might be trying to meditate to help with some pressing problem, so our internal thought loop may sound something like this: *I'm going to sit here and relax my mind ... but I've got to pay that overdue bill before they shut off my lights! How can I "relax" my thoughts when I'm worried about paying my ...*

You can stop right there, because this train of thought is something that you're familiar with, isn't it? Unwanted thoughts often consist of harsh inventories or imaginary disaster scenarios that want to play over and over in your mind. That's okay—let the disastrous scenario play itself all the way through, then start it over and about halfway in, stop it and say to yourself: *Wait a minute ... that's my "I Have to Pay My Bills" thought loop. I recognize it, and I really don't need to go there right now—it doesn't do anything for me except make me upset. I'll avoid replaying that predictable thought loop for now and go back to a calm, comfortable place in my mind.*

Don't suppress, or avoid these specific arising thoughts—they're there for a reason. Don't cling to them or attach your feelings to them, because that same thought loop will very likely start right up again. Simply objectify it, witness it, analyze it, and dismiss it again—as many times as you need to (until you overcome it). That's analytical meditation, because it teaches you to analytically objectify and *witness* your thought process as something separate from the authentic *you*.

The more you witness your thought process this way, the easier it becomes to avoid, pause, fast-forward, or replay thought loops. As we witness when those thoughts arise, the forms they take and the feelings they give us, we get better and better at refocusing (or *un-focusing*) our mind away from them. We "still our flame," "smooth out our pond," or "wipe our mirror clean." We gain more control and begin to discover and create *space* in our thought process where those automatic loops used to run wild. We can start to be a conductor of our thoughts and aim our thinking process at problem-solving if we want, or simply seek the calm space *in between* our thoughts. We no longer have to follow our mind like a hapless carriage driver behind a team of runaway horses.

Another good place to start is to softly keep one small thought in single-pointed focus, like *I only have this one small thought…I only have this one small thought…I only have this one small thought…* Breathe evenly, and continue to return to this central, controlled "one small thought" until it fades or you turn it off and experience the calm space where it used to be.

The analytical revelation in this technique is this: If I am not that demanding thought-stream, if I can witness it, avoid it, change its direction, refocus it—if I can observe it and objectively manipulate it—then just *who is doing the witnessing?* When you stop identifying yourself with your restless thought process, you can identify with a deeper, more encompassing mind. You're suddenly free to think the way angels think. The *who* in that equation is your *authentic* self. It's the *I am* part of the sentence that's connected to everything in a place of calm reason (a place of light and Love).

When you get really good at this form of meditation, you can direct your mind to rest in the calm space *in between thoughts*. For me, it's a little like holding my breath—arresting my thought process right in the middle of the eternal moment. In that place, you can even (however briefly) figuratively slip your head through a narrow window into a dimension of illumination where you experience what Hindus call *samadhi*, what Buddhists call *bodhi*, what Gnostics call *gnosis*, and what Sufis call *fana*. We might know it best as *Unified Consciousness*, but for our own special purpose, for now, let's just say you can see the light of Heaven.

2) Devotional Meditation

It's always helpful to focus on a peaceful, even "holy," place in our mind when we meditate. We can call up thoughts and feelings of a divine environment or of an inspirational spiritual figure. The goal of this approach to meditation is to consciously experience the atmosphere of Love generated by a revered place or person, so it's important to allow ourselves to *feel deeply* and to expand from our hearts. We might single-pointedly focus on a heavenly dimension, a sacred location, a perfect summer day, a stately oak tree in a meadow, or on a prophet, saint, or catalyst of personal transformation, like Jesus, Buddha, Mother Mary, Mahatma Gandhi, or whoever stands out as a central spiritual example in your life.

We can focus on our personal concept of God: the Heavenly Father, the Feminine Divine, the Miraculous Universe, the Synchronistic Quantum Matrix, and so forth. We might center our meditative thoughts and feelings directly on the presence of Love in the eternal moment. We may focus on Love as gratitude—for the gifts we receive each day, for the opportunities we have for sharing our joys and sorrows with one another. We can direct our thoughts to the flow of Love through our lives, or on the simple truth that everyone and everything deserves Love. Our internal dialogue then might go something like this, for example:

"Thank you, God [Divine Mother, Jesus, Buddha, Krishna, angels and ancestors, family and friends], for the Love in my life. Make me a pure channel of Love and Peace. Let Love surround me and flow through me. Let me sit in a place of Love and light. Let me *be Love*."

As you say this, keep your single-pointed focus on the subject of your purest spiritual devotion. You may imagine sitting *with* your devotional figure—directly across from the Buddha, say, or with Jesus standing behind you, resting his hands on your shoulders.

You may pray or chant to focus your meditation with the energy of your object of devotion. Chant the word *Om*—open "ahhh," then out and rounded "O," and ending with a deep *mmmmm*—and the vibratory tone of the sacred word will actually bring your vibrations into alignment with the Universe. It works with any reverential incantation, such as the Lord's Prayer, the Prayer of Saint Francis, or a mantra, like *om mani padme hoong*—the Avalokiteshvara Buddha's mantra of Love and great compassion. We can call on the spirits of light and Love that surround us, or invoke the power of the Universe that makes the sun shine and the flowers bloom. We can single-pointedly focus on that power to help us bloom into Love, or to disassemble our material fears into the loving fold of Time and Space alive in the eternal moment. That is blissful *presence*—that is, "annihilation" into the Divine.

With this easy devotional focus we forget *ourselves* and the troubled thoughts of our unconscious ego, and connect to our *authentic* selves in the beauty and mystery of Unified Divine Consciousness. We spontaneously recognize ourselves as being one with everybody and everything, and transcend mundane fears and superficial demands, transformed by the quality of Love's grounding energy. We can erase our thinking at the finite level of self-centeredness and experience our heart energy expanding into the infinite field of Love.

3) Physical Meditation

What do you see when you have your eyes closed? It's not pure blackness, is it? In fact, there's a kind of field of waving, effervescent light there inside your eyelids—dim, vibrating, *alive*. There's a sort of dance of particles, the lack of light (or the remains of light) creating fields of color and energy that erupt and wave across your inner vision. It's a kind of elemental connection that you actually witness with your eyes closed. It's not just a dark nothing in there, is it?

What makes you breathe and makes your heart beat? It's totally *involuntary*, totally intuitive. We could say that it's the same power that's behind the heartbeat of the Universe—the pulsing evidence of the very moment of Creation—and we'd be absolutely right on that score. While even the best efforts of our intellect can't describe this miracle, just sit quietly and concentrate on your breathing, and you'll find yourself immediately grounded in it—the inexplicable processes of our animation, the magical experience of Being, the drumbeat of Life.

You breathe in, the breath makes its cycle, then you breathe out, a small space occurs, and then you breathe in again. You may focus on the action by counting your breaths, but whether you do or not, you'll begin to notice that your material thought-forms dissipate, and little else enters your internal dialogue when you concentrate on this simple, natural process. Your directed thoughts might go something like this: *I breathe in slowly through my nose, my breath turns the corner, and I breathe out slowly through my mouth … in through my nose, out through my mouth … in deeply, out slowly.*

You can broaden the physical effect by assigning conscious meaning and intention to your actions, such as *I breathe in again from my stomach, drawing in the sky, and breathe out down through my hips, anchoring to the Earth.*

Or you can do what the Tibetans call *tonglen*, an action-based "giving and taking" meditation where we breathe in the pain all around us, and breathe out loving kindness: *I take in all the suffering of the Earth and its inhabitants, and I release pure loving heart-energy.*

As you sit, breathe in and out, develop a single-pointed focus, direct your thoughts toward a purposeful realization, and simply *be* alive and awake in the moment, you'll find aspects of these three approaches merge together, as they should. Conscious awareness of *analytical meditation* enters your inner dialogue, and you become more and more adept at controlling your thoughts, so that when fears and unwarranted reactions arise, you can avoid or transform them.

You become able to direct your thought process toward Love through *devotional meditation*, as you sustain the graceful unifying thought: *I am alive in everything and everything lives in me; I am light, I am Love.*

In *physical meditation* you can watch the energy cascade across your inner screen, breathe with the Universe, and realize a blissful surrender into the extra-dimension of Unified Consciousness that enfolds, supports, and animates everything.

Listening to Heaven in Meditation

Eventually, as you sit in the comfort of your more spacious mind, you may begin to hear the voice of an intuitive intelligence arise from beyond your immediate, self-generated thoughts—a calm, sane, benevolent intelligence, superior to your own. You may have heard this intelligence before, perhaps at times when you felt lost and a little hopeless, when it said things to you like *it's all going to be all right*, or when you felt torn by a difficult choice and it said *don't go that way, come this way*. Almost every time you trusted your gut, that inner voice was right. As you meditate more deeply, you will begin to notice a *channel* opening up within you—a crack in the surface of this reality that allows you to contact a greater, more graceful intelligence in the form of *the voices of your spirit guides*. You will actually begin to hear the voices of your angels and ancestors talking to you—no kidding.

If you open your heart to these possibilities, a meditative miracle available to everyone who faithfully does the work will allow you to access a limitless well of intuitive intelligence, and to realize that you actually do have guardian angels available to you.

Does that sound a little crazy to you? Would it just be your imagination? If so, that's okay too, because imagination is a powerful channel to that benevolent, innovative intelligence. In fact, *it's all the same thing*—your ego just wants to label it as "unrealistic" again. A good way to test this truth is that if you investigate it objectively, you'll find that calm inner intelligence, what the Quakers call "the still, small voice," is never wrong. You may interpret it wrongly or wishfully, but when you're totally honest with yourself, you'll know that the truth has been there all along.

Personally, for a long time I didn't want to hear about extra-dimensional voices speaking to me from beyond. Until I became a regular meditator, I scarcely even acknowledged that *I had not been alone* during each of my three episodes of near death—and even then it wasn't my idea! My guardian angel came to me in meditation one day and introduced herself (even though I'd been "hearing" her for years). I know this is true in my life because I've accumulated a lot of undeniable evidence. My angels are frequently right when I am not, they come up with much better ideas than I do on my own, and they regularly provide remarkable, spontaneous insights—all of which is real evidence for why I have faith in them.

The willingness to meditate is the only key you need to open this channel to the miraculous. Learn to listen to your intuition, and allow your faith in it to grow, because then whatever questions you ask with sincerity and open-heartedness (in "prayer") will be answered in meditation.

It's like having a life coach drop in on you from Heaven.

Moving Through Obstacles with Meditation

I hope that these techniques are helpful—they're the best I can do to describe what has worked for me to regularly experience the extra-dimensional reality that I felt a part of in my three NDEs. I always go back to this wonderful observation made by the Buddha when he was asked "What have you gained from all your meditation?"

"Nothing at all," he replied.

"Then what good is it?"

"Let me tell you what I *lost* through meditation: sickness, anger, depression, insecurity, the burden of old age, the fear of death. That is the good of meditation, which leads to nirvana." [27]

Teachers from the East, like the Buddha, have served as models for wisdom teachers in popular media, like the remarkable twenti-

---

27. Easwaran, *The Dhammapada*, 58.

eth-century guru Sri Aurobindo, when he teaches us some benefits of meditation and foreshadows the mystical heart of a pop phenomenon like *Star Wars*: "The important thing is to get rid of the habit of the invasion of troubling thoughts, wrong feelings, confusion of ideas, unhappy movements. These disturb the nature and cloud it and make it difficult for the Force to work. When the mind is quiet and at peace, the Force can work more easily. It should be possible to see things that have to be changed in you without being upset or depressed; the change is then more easily done."[28]

Some of the most practical personal benefits come from meditation when you become like a deep-sea diver into yourself. Once you are able to clear space in your thoughts and calmly submerge in levels of your own consciousness, then you can really start exploring, because meditation will allow you (probably for the first time ever) to dive down into your subconscious, and even into your unconscious at times, and witness it with actual awareness.

All of us have those submerged experiences in our past—childhood incidents, traumatic episodes, or losses and regrets that we just can't seem to shake. The effects of these experiences may continue showing up in our lives as difficult issues or habits, as obstacles on our path to realizing happiness and wholeness. In the meditative state, when we're sitting in that presence of the eternal moment, we can begin to really look at those issues with the kind of single-pointed focus that we get from stilling our flame, or smoothing the surface of our pond. At first, the shape of the obstacle rises up before us, and then its features develop and begin to sharpen—the troubled face of a relative, the courtyard of our high school, that embarrassing moment during the holidays years ago.

Like in my second NDE, when I was shown those vital moments from my life, meditative presence disengages us from Time and Space and lets a moment come into focus—viewable from the perspective of a spiritual witness. As you focus on the moment in your heart, *you can see what really happened, and why it is continuing to color your life.* In

---

28. Aurobindo, *Bases of Yoga*, 2.

the clarity of meditative presence, there's no context for dishonesty or misrepresentation—there's no more ego-self to fool. You're able to witness "the dance of what is"—the way that obstacle came to be, and what it does to you. You can reexperience the source of your suffering right in front of you. Like a diver finding an oyster, inside that moment is the point of irritation that's caused the pain, and centered in it (holding it in your hands) *you can pry it open,* and in its tender heart you'll find the precious reward for all the troubles you've put yourself through.

That realization is a pearl of authenticity—the *I am deserving of Love and happiness* moment that encapsulates your trauma and dissolves the pain, making it possible to bring that long-hidden part of yourself out into the light and to help reveal your life's purpose.

Meeting Your Challenges, Facing the Wilderness

I love to meditate outside in nature, and the idea of sitting in the wilderness has always had a metaphoric power too, where the "wilderness" stands for this challenging world we inhabit. Two of my favorite meditation teachers, the Buddha and Jesus, sat in the wilderness as a means to realizing enlightenment, Christhood, and the direction of their true purpose. They needed to overcome all delusions of separateness, all the obstacles that prevented them from unifying themselves with the power of Love—and they did it by meditating.

Both of them, sitting in nature, were met by three tenacious categories of our own suffering, the obstacles that stand in the way of realizing Heaven in our lives. Each challenge arose when they discovered they *weren't really alone* out there, that there was another (inner) personality sitting in the wild with them—the antagonistic aspect of human nature that we've been calling the *ego-mind.* The Buddha knew him as *Mara,* the tempter, and to Jesus, of course, he was just good old, bad old *Satan.*

It's not much of a stretch to realize these two antagonists as personifications of our instinctive ego—the host of the three "temptations" that stood between our teachers and their realization of

Heaven on Earth. Let's look at those stubborn obstacles so that we, too, might dissolve them through meditation:

1. The desire to control things to be just the way we want them to be—to effectively be completely in charge of our own world.

2. The material and physical satisfactions that we desire to have gratified—the elusive rewards and entitlements that sometimes feel like our "only" reasons to live.

3. Our unavoidable *fears*—usually having to do with the idea of losing, or never getting, the control or gratification we defined in numbers one and two.

In the depth of the Buddha's meditation to enlightenment, Mara provocatively suggested to him that he deserved to be the king of the entire realm,[29] much like when Jesus sat in the wilderness and the devil offered him "dominion over all."[30]

Wouldn't any of us love to be able to exert complete control over our world, to have the ability to make reality conform to our wishes? Buddha and Jesus recognized that this unrealistic offer was only attractive to their ego and so they humbly refused, surrendering ambition to a divinely conscious power they could have faith in, instead of seeking to control. Our meditation gives us the opportunity to realize that the world is fine without our needing to control it, and to strategically surrender to the benevolent forces that direct our lives. Only the *karma* we create and resolve—the choices we make—can actually determine the state of our serenity.

Sitting in your wilderness helps develop a naturally healthy ego, free from the idea that something *more* will improve your life, when you really have everything you need already. This was the next temptation that Buddha and Jesus were confronted with: the insistent impulse that selfish gratification—luxurious surroundings, extravagant meals, grand acknowledgments, sexual satisfactions, etc.—will

---

29. Asvaghosa, *The Buddha-Carita*, 165.
30. Luke 4:5,6.

somehow make us whole and happy. There's one big problem with that formula: sensory gratification evaporates in the eternal moment. Meditation helps us realize a more lasting definition of success—one based in fulfilling the needs of others, in a grounded serenity, and in a more authentic relationship to Life, instead of seeking one elusive "fix" after another. The solution is meditation, not *medication*. Health and fulfillment are only generated in moments of real presence, and can never be permanently captured by pursuing ever-changing sensations.

The ultimate challenge to our wilderness meditators was also the most stubborn, and it's simply the phenomenon of *fear*: the fear of undeserved consequences and unfulfilled desires; the fear of not measuring up; the fear of being unloved or left behind; the fear of death. Mara sent an army of fierce warriors thundering at Siddhartha as he sat beneath the Bodhi Tree, filling the air with a barrage of pointy fears aimed straight at him—but *those fears weren't real*. Fears are only shadow aspects of an insecure ego that dissolve in the truthful radiance of meditation. As the barrage of spears and arrows bore down on Siddhartha, he touched the Earth and instantly personified the unity of all Life. The spears and arrows turned to flowers that rained down all around him, and in that eternal moment he became the Buddha.

The lesson is that you are always taken care of in the eternal moment. Fear is not real, unless you concede to give it that power. Death is merely a required part of growing through Life. These may sound like well-intended solicitudes now, but after practicing some meditation they'll become statements of truth for you too.

I'm not suggesting that you can become a Buddha or a Christ, but you can head out into the wilderness yourself to sit on a rock by the river, or on a misty mountain top, or on a backyard patch of grass—or even on a pillow in your bedroom. In a wilderness where the human unconsciousness is the most terrifying force known, disarming our ego temptations is essential for our return to the shelter of Love.

EXERCISE: *Guiding Yourself to Bliss*

There are already a number of exercises suggested in the forms of meditation that I've become familiar with and passed along here, except one, which is a whole lot of fun, and will not only help you discover what works best for you, but will also help you formulate your idea of what you want your Heaven to look like. It's *self-guided meditation*, and I'll give you an example of how it works for me.

I get myself ready to sit, perhaps with a candle and a gentle soundtrack. I close my eyes and picture myself walking down a path through a beautiful tropical forest. The powdery dirt beneath my bare feet is warm and soft. It's dusk, and as the trail opens up to a placid lagoon, I sit in my half-lotus in about an inch of warm, calm water. The late evening sunset reflects off the pool as the water slowly rises above my hips. The stars come out as the sky darkens into a deep blue, and as the lattice of bright stars overhead reflects off the glassy surface of the water, I feel completely surrounded by stars—like jewels are suspended around me in a cosmic web, with all the jewel-like stars reflecting their many sparkling facets. As the warm water rises, I gently drift down through the warm, breathable liquid into a soft, secure evening darkness, and come to rest serene and whole, surrounded by my underwater lattice of gently pulsing sparks of the Divine, filled with, and completely a part of, Love.

That's one of mine—now make up one of your own!

- 13 -
Recognize the Sacred
in Everything:
... and (Surprise!) Become a
Whole Lot Happier

It's been suggested by wiser people than I that you can choose to view the Universe in one of two ways: as though nothing is particularly miraculous or as though *everything* is. By this time, I'm sure you know which of those two directions I go in. I've had a few too many miracles happen to me personally (whether I asked for them or not), as I'm sure we probably all have had. Once we start to develop the eyes to see the miraculous nature of Life, we can't help but begin to notice the Sacred in every direction we look. You look at the stars and are overwhelmed by the grandeur and the mathematical unlikeliness of all of life on Earth—that's a sacred design. You look at the green life that germinates in the ground, and when you finally sit down to eat those beautiful vegetables from the garden, you know that's sacred too.

If you've ever been present for a birth or a death, you know that at those moments we occupy an indescribably sacred "bubble"—a timeless space, transformed by the presence of the Divine, coalescing into a miraculous passage of *being*. In an instant a baby makes its first sound—a tiny human setting off on an entire life. In that same instant a spirit tangibly exits a body and leaves lifeless matter behind as a quantum spark of unique expression escapes into a different dimension. We all marvel with faux expertise at the miracle of a baby being born—like we know what's going on—but meanwhile, growing evidence supports an extra-dimensional exchange at the other end of life too. The real experience of witnessing these sacred birth and death phenomena can transform even the most diehard skeptic.

The More Your Eyes Open, the More Sacred You See

Caught up in day-to-day life, it's easy to overlook the miraculous nature of *everything* (especially in the morning before our first miraculous cup of coffee), but all we have to do is be present for one moment and there it is again, pouring out in every direction we look. Unconsciousness clings onto its defenses, but when you're really honest with yourself and recognize the undeniable interconnectedness of all Life, it's hard not to appreciate the concept called *pantheism*, the idea that absolutely everything is a manifestation of the Divine.

If you've been practicing the spiritually perspective-enhancing principles from the first chapters (kindness, humility, honesty, forgiveness, compassion, and service), you have probably noticed something happening as a result of your changing view of Life—the undeniable connection that changes you forever.

This is the realization that *it deeply hurts you to cause pain.* Causing injury to another sentient creature creates bad karma for you, and effectively causes an injury to yourself. You begin to notice that when you say something that isn't particularly thoughtful or considerate, it just *sounds wrong* to you. Like spilled coffee on a clean white shirt, you can't wear it well—your ego may want you to conceal it, but your true self knows you need to quickly blot it out. Soon, small things that never mattered before come alive in your conscience. When you see a person being wasteful or exploitative, being a bully or a braggart, you sense the energy of injustice, of insecurity, of pain; and you increasingly feel like intervening somehow to possibly correct the impropriety. Pretty soon you're capturing bugs in a jar and releasing them out the back door saying *Go be free, my little bug friend.*

You may start feeling a little out of place from the growing sensitivity to your surroundings, but this perceptual and behavioral change is really a very good thing. When you notice the harm you can do to Life when you're not conscious of your actions, it means you're beginning to develop the sensibilities of an angel. You're beginning to see and feel what Heaven looks and feels like.

In India, there's an ancient religion called *Jainism,* and the Jains are so attuned to living life this way that they absolutely must not cause harm to anything. They sweep their walkways with extra soft brooms to prevent anyone from stepping on a bug, and wear extra loose clothes so as not to injure any insects in tight folds. The Jains' consideration extends to life that's so small it isn't visible, suggesting that even the tiniest organisms and living vibrations are sacred entities, deserving respect and compassion. This practice, called *ahimsa*—absolute non-violence and non-injury—was the inspiration for Mahatma Gandhi's approach to liberating India from British rule, so it ought to work for the liberation of our souls too. The Jains' chief purpose is just that: to recognize and be of help to every eternal soul.

If you're having those uneasy feelings arise, or hearing a still, small voice of reason gently advising you against causing harm, meditate on it and you'll realize that it's the voice of your intuitive intelligence simply directing you *how to live.* It means that you're beginning to hear the Life instructions that arise from your heart, which is your onboard receiver and transmitter of the Sacred. Your personal consciousness is expanding into extra-dimensional Consciousness. Your angels are talking to you, and now you can hear them. Sometimes it's not really a voice so much as an intuitive feeling that arises out of palpable energies—"fluctuations in the Force," as they say in *Star Wars.* The perception of those energies is a very real thing, and a very good sign that an impulse for heavenly goodness is growing within you.

If something doesn't *feel* right in a room, or if you sense the presence of suffering in the attitude or aura of a friend, don't doubt it.

Those energies are real, and usually you'll intuitively know how much Love you need to help you find a solution. When you allow that perception, that sensibility, to expand, you begin to see how energies are transmittable, communicable, and how they can be passed along in very direct or very subtle ways. This all means that you're *waking up*.

The ability to recognize the Sacred manifests itself in the ability to perceive the light and Love emanating out of the material forms that surround you, made apparent by the "annihilation" of your ego-self into the Divine Mystery. Now we're talking about how we are actually participating in Unified Consciousness. By engaging our *Self* in the larger field of shared Consciousness with awareness, we can engage with the actual energy of Consciousness present in a room, in a crowd, or even in a region or nation; in the Consciousness alive in the energies and sensations in Mother Nature or with the entire Consciousness of the Earth, as an experience we share with everything alive on our planet. We develop the awareness of our sixth sense.

Let's get really basic and follow this natural intuition down to its most elemental levels for a moment. For example, within our deepest patterns of Consciousness formation, we all have a real sense of the elemental forces of the Earth: the crystalline cold of the polar subterranean; the heedless baking of the equatorial sun; the smoldering heat and pressure of the innermost core. In a way, we can know those sensations immediately, beneath the level of our imaginations, when we simply enter into the eternal moment and focus our attention there. As we begin climbing back up toward the light of pure Unified Consciousness, there are discoveries we need to make while reentering a state of compassionate identification with more complex forms of Life. Engaged in our expedition in upward Consciousness, we can't help but identify with all the other creatures along the way up the food chain.

The Sacred Reality of All Life on Earth

It isn't only humans who experience the thin veneer of Consciousness that tenderly wraps and energetically enlivens this planet; it's all of life on Earth. Despite our differences, from species to species we are all one thing: *the Consciousness alive on this Earth*. We all intimately share that Sacred Reality. Deep within us, we know the natural experience of all of Life. We can reach down and feel the elements as any animal does, and relate to any animal, living the play of forces that governs our need for sustenance, for regeneration, for Love in the form of the mysterious power of creation, and in the ways we must satisfy those needs through our temporal form.

In our ego-mind, we humans tend to think of ourselves as being at the top of the food chain, but we're not. In reality, the *Earth* is the living entity at the top of the food chain, as it will swallow up every one of us. Where our sensory capabilities actually put us in the sacred order of things is in our potential and expression for stewardship. Animals don't exist to bring conscious spiritual evolution into the world, because as the uniquely articulated channels we are, that's what humans are for. We are here with the primary purpose of promoting the spiritual evolution of Life on Earth. Ours is not the sacred power to determine what lives and dies—everything does that already, including ourselves; ours is actually the power to express intelligent creativity and responsible, compassionate stewardship.

Anyone with anxieties can sense a Divine serenity landing in their lap when a cat jumps up and settles in for a snuggle. The energy of the Sacred expressing itself through the cat (Love) will heal their anxiety because the animal is a direct channel to the Divine. The animal's authentic nature is often unabashedly joyous and playful too. Lions romp like kittens, birds sometimes clearly fly for fun, and our pets at home can always get up and insist that we have a good time. The point of experiencing Consciousness is to enjoy it, and our kindred animals, of all different species, give us great examples of the power that play brings to the experience of Life. The authentic spiritual connection with our shared Source is innocently joyful, open-hearted, and intuitively grateful.

The cognitive dissonance of our ego-minds commonly concludes that animals have limited conscious experience of Life, but actually that's not true at all. Science continues to prove greater degrees of animal intelligence than many people are comfortable considering. As I mentioned earlier, because of this unwillingness to recognize the profound intelligence alive in the sentience of other creatures—as they express the Sacred through their own uniquely tailored engagements with Consciousness—the human ego selfishly denies other creatures their rightful place in the hierarchy of being. It suggests a spiritually fatal assumption of human "intelligence": that as the top of a "divine" order of our own imagining, we have the right to exploit or kill animals for whatever purpose we wish. This misunderstanding creates a tragic obstacle to our spiritual evolution.

First Nation, indigenous people have always had an appropriately respectful relationship to the sacred nature of animals—particularly those they create an interdependence with. They honor their sacred bond with ritual, stewardship, and spiritual responsibility. They engage in "the Great Spirit" as partners with the animals, assuming a kind of sacred parity with one another, where they identify themselves with the animal and merge their spirits together. They both need their relationship, not only for sustenance but also for their own expressions of the Divine—it's a spiritually symbiotic, interdependent balance that they've agreed upon naturally, a mutual recognition of the sacred energies of the Earth.

A powerful earthquake doesn't care about the presumed superiority of human beings, yet the energy of the Earth reliably notifies animals of impending catastrophes. Elephants head for the hills well before the tsunami strikes shore, as do most creatures. This is because a recognition of "non-ordinary" energies (the powers employed by the invisible machinery of Life) is part of the sensory capability of many animals to connect directly to Source. We humans naturally have it too, as a sixth sense that manifests as forms of transpersonal communication, synchronicity, clairvoyance and clairsentience, remote viewing, interspecies communication, and many other such non-ordinary forms of awareness. We often can't tune it in like other creatures do naturally, because our insistent ego-interface wants to interpret everything as being right or wrong and ends up suppressing this whole field of our potential. But we can improve our recognition by paying attention in a mindful way.

How to Recognize the Sacred

Everything in the material world is shifting energy in material form, and living things are especially sensitive examples of this. The Love-based or fear-based energies we follow and project into our surroundings are reflected back to us in the conditions of our living world. We are individually shifted and formed by that energetic dynamic at our most basic level, as is all other life on the planet. Being the creatures that have more effect on the world than any others, we have to consciously reject destructive ego, follow our intuitive intelligence, and seek expressions of Love to foster and expand the most beneficial energies possible. Steadfast recognition of the Sacred in all of Life inspires our alignment with those beneficial energies in the most direct and natural way. For example, Love, as you might imagine, has everything to do with forms of Heaven, while fear doesn't. Animals may briefly experience the energy of fear in the moment as an inspiration for survival, but humans alone have the unique ability to experience fear in the past tense and to project fearful energy into the future—to form and create energies of discord and imbalance.

When we inculcate domesticated animals with the energy of fear, the animals, being divinely sensitive energy channels, absorb the energy of fear on an elemental, cellular level. As we ignore the Sacred in those creatures and are complicit in their exploitation, then when we consume them, we consume the energy of cumulative fear, and continue to cycle it though our very being, where it continues to disable our ability to recognize the Sacred. Suppressed shame and self-hatred for our betrayal of the Sacred—the denial of our true level of spiritual evolution—is powerfully recycled into our psyches. It cripples our spiritual potential as *cognitive dissonance* critically obstructs our ability to realize our sixth-sensory awareness, the dimension of Love we live within, and the potential cooperative grace of *Heaven on Earth*. The continued destruction of wildlife and natural habitat further accelerates this global imbalance.

Our continued misuse of the sacred expression of animals to feed our needs is quite harmful to our spiritual growth and realization. This idea may sound extreme to you, but you can test it within yourself. Does it make you uncomfortable to seriously consider livestock factory conditions and methods of animal breeding and slaughter? Look it up, focus on the actual techniques, and honestly consider it in your own experience, and if it makes you uncomfortable at all, you'll know that you're doing spiritual damage to yourself. You're making it virtually impossible to realize the graceful potential of Life that's available to us all when we recognize and respect the Sacred in all things.

Overlooking this potential is easy when we don't recognize the Divine Nature of Life, but many of us don't think we can live any other way. Acknowledging the Sacred in all things brings a saner and more spiritually responsible way of living to light. For example, the big beautiful steer we feel we must rely on for a source of protein got big and beautiful by eating grass, so a more rational option, on every level, is to do what benefits *all* Life, and try switching to a vegetable protein–based diet. If it's too big a leap at first, then take it a little at a time. Look for providers who practice compassionate methods of raising livestock—who treat, pasture, and feed animals in humanely natural, spiritually evolved ways. Look at this issue from a spiritual perspective—primarily as a respecter of Life, then as a responsible steward of the planet.

Proof of this improved reality exists in embodying all the benefits that a vegan or vegetarian lifestyle can bring. Not only will you always have more and better energy pouring through your body, and be physically much healthier by every available measure, but you'll also likely live a lot longer. You'll find it easier to maintain a better attitude, to find Love, and to be happy—free from the subconscious guilt of participating in any unnecessary exploitation of the Sacred. Instead, you'll elevate your spiritual well-being by consciously celebrating it in every form. It's the single best way you can personally address the extreme environmental destruction and waste that animal exploitation inarguably generates, and you'll comfortably contribute to the recovery of the environment and the spiritual balance of the world.

Recognizing all the forms of the Sacred allows you to live in a state of grace that you never imagined possible before, and to exercise a compassionate Consciousness and awareness that will transform your personal world—and will contribute to the heavenly restoration of the Earth, as it was given to us. It also gives you a vitalized sense of divine responsibility that can fully and intuitively inform your life, enabling you to *stand up* when you need to, to contribute to the balance of the planet meaningfully with Love, and to create divine, living realities out of formerly lifeless wastelands. You'll align yourself with the Sacred, and by doing so, become one with the Sacred yourself.

EXERCISE: *Recognize the Sacred in Everything*

There are a couple of very simple exercises to help you recognize the Sacred in everything (as if you needed any help). One is that when you go on your next outing, just notice *everything* along the way, and acknowledge it, like so: *Hello, tree! Hello, rock! Hello, bench! Hello, dog!* You can immediately become aware of how much light and Love and vitality comes pouring through different forms. The energy you get back directly informs you as to the level of sentient Consciousness each form is channeling; it will become increasingly obvious, because some dogs just sit there expressionless, while some trees definitely *want a hug!*

You can also walk around the supermarket and open your heart to recognizing the Sacred in everything you see and feel there. In many countries the outdoor public markets are full of it, while in the United States you can find it mostly by walking around the outside edge of the store. Stop in front of departments—packaged foods, produce, the butcher—and open up to the energies of vitality, light and Love, and healthfulness, as well as to those of toxicity, violence, and consumerism.

The Sacred, as it will reflect itself to you in your heart, will point you in the direction toward Heaven.

– 14 –
Look for the Divine in Others:
Realizing Heavenly Relationships

Now that we've investigated a better way of looking at the world and all our fellow creatures through the filter of the Divine, let's return to our first imaginary experience of *spiritual perspective* for a moment, and consider how employing it might help us get along better with one another.

Picture yourself in a big room full of people going about their business—maybe an office, or a department store. Now imagine that you've become unstuck from your body—your spirit slips out of your physical self and drifts up above the crowd, up near the ceiling. From that perspective you can see everybody intently involved in whatever they're doing down there. You witness the physicality of our human forms—the vehicles of "soft machinery" that our consciousness rides around in. People *have to be* human down there—don't they?— in order to act out their impulses and desires and duties, constantly experiencing the input of their senses and the stream of feelings that define all their different forms of expressing Consciousness. Some have expressions of grim intention, some are buoyant and carefree, some look like they're somewhere else, while others are acting out or laughing out loud. Everyone is different, yet everyone is simultaneously engaging in the field of shared Consciousness in exactly the same way, through their own vehicles, which are all roughly the equivalent of everyone else's.

Which of them could be your friends? Which could be your family? Who, down there, do you feel like you could get along with? Who are you attracted to? Who is nearly invisible to you? Who would you avoid at all costs? And why?

In Heaven, there are all kinds of spirits, all light and Love energy, all occurring simultaneously. They're no longer challenged or defined by the constraints of earthly form. Everyone knows *they all are really an expression of the Divine,* in their own different ways. They recognize those little differences—their quirks and peccadillos—as being little flaws that they all have, so everyone gets along very well. Since we're still just human beings in a constant struggle to return to the light, assuming that heavenly perspective of tolerance and equanimity is a good place for us to start.

Be Love, Not Judgment

By this time we're used to looking at life in different ways than before, so when we look at our relationship to others, we need to bring all of those lessons front and center. From our spiritual perspective, through the filter of the Divine, everyone is a luminous energy being riding around in fragile physical vehicles that range from rather graceful and "attractive" to possibly more challenged or "less attractive." Looking through heavenly eyes it's all beautiful. The real nature of our interactions has to start with that essential identification with our human form: *We are all the same thing, in slightly different forms, expressing the infinite Consciousness we share.*

We all have the same thoughts, worries, demands, joys, emotions, and hopes—more or less. We're clearly all the same thing, but busily being human makes it a challenge to keep that in mind. We've got so much on our plate already that even though we know unconditional Love is the answer to our troubles, surrendering to that spiritual purpose can easily be overlooked.

For some persistent, counterproductive reason, my ego-mind can be willing to label everyone I meet as some kind of potential threat (part of its prehistoric habit, I guess). Luckily, I'm often able to avoid the pain that thought process can create, and redirect the energy. It's a conscious awareness that can take those insensitive, default labels, like *That man is overweight; That guy looks like a rich kid; That girl is plain; That woman has a bad attitude,* and reveal my defensive motivations by turning them into honest questions about myself, like *Am I being vain or uncompassionate? Do I have financial fears? Am I judging a book by its cover? Am I really unwilling to help that struggling woman?*

Catching myself applying labels that way helps me ask myself why I'd automatically be thinking such things about someone I don't know. Am I projecting one of my own fearful defects onto an unsuspecting recipient? There's almost always some unnecessary fear or self-doubt conditioning those spontaneous snap judgments, so that my selfish ego is actually doing me a favor—it's telling me where to start looking for my own problems. "Everything that irritates us about others can lead us to a better understanding of ourselves," wisely suggested our old friend Dr. Carl Jung.[31]

Once again, it's our discomforts that point out the adjustments we need to make, so we can get to know ourselves better and be more respectful of others. Having a healthy, self-deprecating sense of humor about our own flaws puts us on the common ground of kindness that opens us to sharing more fun in our interactions. Our egos can keep things very serious, but our authentic selves always percolate with an open-hearted joyfulness that we can project toward everyone we meet and inject into every situation we share. *We can have fun with each other.* Projecting fun and optimism defines any circumstance in a way that opens our hearts to joyful relationships with complete strangers, before we even meet them.

A Guide to Heavenly Relationships: Use the Simple Principles

Let's recap the life principles that serve as the guides to how to treat everyone we meet, the way everyone treats everyone else in Heaven.

---

31. Jung, *Memories, Dreams, Reflections,* 247.

When we sincerely show *kindness* to people, we activate an invisible field of camaraderie—the field of Love—that creates kindness in return. We realize that we're part of a "secret" spiritual club, and that a friendly conspiracy can direct our relationship from there on. There's also a wink and nod that joyful identification with one another makes possible... that this can always be more *fun* than I thought it would be.

When we demonstrate *humility*, people let their protective guard down, because we don't project the desire to be better than anyone else. We can have relaxed, authentic relationships because instead of competing in some subtle or not-so-subtle way, we're identifying with mutually respectful and beneficial intention.

When we exhibit *honesty*, many people are shocked—in a nice way, of course! This life inures us to so much insincerity that meeting a truly honest person is a real blessing, an encouragement of life's most valuable qualities. Being honest invites honesty from others, resulting in more authentic, dependable relationships. Honesty is fun too, because it can't help but inspire a little self-deprecating humor, especially when we share the same silly stuff that bothers all of us. (*I hate when I do that...*)

Automatically showing *forgiveness* allows us to let the little stuff slide. Who cares anyway, in this great big world? If we don't exploit one another's vulnerabilities but identify with them instead, we enter into a special relationship with one another, by recognizing that holding on to little difficulties causes everyone unnecessary pain.

When we have *compassion* in our hearts, we create a whole different level of fellowship based in the solid, caring intelligence that's alive in the field of Love—not the fearful sense of separation our prehistoric egos tend to promote so seriously. We develop loving restraint and acceptance and become willing to bring unconditional Love in, without expecting anything in return.

It all leads to the willingness to be of *service* to others, without any wish for acknowledgment or compensation—giving unconditional Love also gives the giver the greatest gift of all. We are freed from the bondage of self, and find a sacred purpose in helping others realize that eternal Love unequivocally binds all of us together.

Additional Guidance: A Template for Living

Maintaining this joyful spiritual perspective is a challenge, but here's a concise, reliable, step-by-step guide to help with your life issues and relationships (and to help you find your own kind of Heaven):

- Acknowledge the fact that you're a complicated human being, subject to the unavoidable faults and failings of your physical form and mental processes.
- Realize that through a conscious connection to our spiritual Source, there's a profound intelligence and sanity available that your ego-mind tries to make you disregard.
- Surrender your ego-mind into that spiritual Source, and invest your faith in that connected, intuitive intelligence that's at work in our lives instead.
- Honestly look at the parts of your life that have caused pain for others and yourself, and determine the causes and possible solutions for them.
- Privately share those painful self-discoveries with your Source and with someone you trust to create forgiveness and a new clarification of your authentic self.
- Realize how those faults may have misdirected your choices and damaged your authentic self, and ask your intuitive intelligence (your guiding angels) to help you make better choices from now on.
- Repair and compensate for the wrongs your faults may have caused others and yourself in the past, by the very best means possible.
- Regularly engage in honest self-examination to increase your conscious awareness; consider the events of your day and correct or compensate for any difficulties you may have caused.

- Engage your spiritual self in the divine field of Unified Consciousness through regular meditation and prayer to develop conscious awareness and a connection with Love.
- Offer to be of selfless service to others in any and every way possible, and then aid them in finding their way to Heaven too.

This template for living comes from one of the most revolutionary spiritual movements in all of human history: a twentieth-century synthesis of spiritual principles and the wisdom of the ages known as the "12 Step Program." Formulated by Bill Wilson and Dr. Bob Smith, a stock speculator and a doctor, respectively, both from Vermont, the two put their heads and hearts together to solve their shared struggles with alcoholism. With a little help from their friends, they wrote the book *Alcoholics Anonymous*—a kind of handbook for the restoration of a healing spirituality.[32] The program derived from it, which has proven so effective in the treatment of alcoholism and drug addiction, has been applied with equal effectiveness to recovery from all kinds of spiritual struggles, dependencies, and addictions—nearly every kind of personal hell imaginable.

By inspiring a spiritual self-discovery through surrender of the ego-mind, honest self-examination, taking principled actions, and being of selfless service, this program has not only helped millions of people overcome their deepest life difficulties and join a kind of covert global spiritual fellowship, but has also helped to define the real differences between religion and spirituality—where divine solutions aren't necessarily found through devotional institutions, but through inward practical disciplines. Regardless of (or incorporating) organized religions and personal beliefs, the path to Heaven suggested here is found by way of shared human experience—a fellowship of shared Divine Consciousness, personal spiritual experience, and principled daily actions.

---

32. Mel B., *New Wine*, 1–8.

Trying Out Your Angel Eyes

When I imagine *inhabiting Heaven,* I sometimes consider what it would feel like to be an angel, and how it would be to return to this world to take up the effort to help earthly human beings get to Heaven too.

Would such an angelic vision allow you to compassionately witness somebody's spirit struggling to reveal itself through all the complicated layers of their human condition? What if we used our imaginations and pretended to be an angel, standing in front of another human being, completely liberated from our ego-mind, compassionate and non-judgmental—how would we perceive a person, meeting them for the first time?

As you first engage with angelic conscious awareness and presence, you may witness their first flash of personality and think, *Ah, here's the spirit that I actually want to meet.* Imagine that first revelation of self-ness, suspending itself in an eternal moment free of Time and Space, and you may spontaneously see the person as the child they once were (and still are, in a way); then you might fast-forward to envision them as an old person—a product of their potential realized. As that perception shakes into the present, your holistic awareness would focus on the complexities of their voice, their body language— the movements of their hands, and their facial expressions, the animation of which would describe their personal expression of Divine Consciousness.

You'd listen and watch with wonder, marveling at the incredible varieties of human *being.* Looking directly into their eyes and paying close, compassionate attention to every word they said, you'd come to the inescapable realization that *this person is me, as I could be inhabiting that form.* Sometimes what they'd be saying to you wouldn't have anything to do with the words coming out of their mouth, while the combination of their spiritual energies and physical expressions might perfectly relate their experience of childhood, accomplishment, trauma, desire, dreams, fears, responsibilities, dietary habits, indoctrinations, and more. It would all instantly add up to the bottom-line energy created by the amount of Love in their formation, how much they're able to transmit, and how much Love they'd be able to receive.

Imagining this ability to see people as an angel would—with that completely objective spiritual perspective and presence—could give us the most profound gift of purposeful understanding that we could possibly have, that *Everyone is trying their best to cope with the world as they know it. Everyone carries their karma with them, reaching back into the experiences of their past, informing this very moment, and projecting into their future. Everyone is living their wishes and needs, their desires, their loves, and their fears—and all with their own internal commentary, all with their own picture of themselves, all at the level of conscious awareness their karma experience has made possible for them to know. Everyone has realized Love to some degree and is able to channel and receive Love as much as their psychic and karmic structures will allow.*

An angel could then celebrate the Love that person carries and projects, and supply what Love is needed to treat whatever hardship the person is expressing—with the open-hearted humor, loving empathy and compassion, tender forgiveness, and selfless support that angels are famous for. That's what they're always doing in Heaven.

Meeting Hard Cases with Compassion

Along our path, we inevitably encounter *difficult* people: people who are not very nice or considerate, who are self-centered and arrogant, dismissive, uncommunicative people who may abuse positions of power, unconsciously make poor decisions, consciously make selfish and destructive decisions, support inhumane causes, behave aggressively or inappropriately—and all the rest that an ego run amok can project. There's a natural instinct to react with some degree of justifiable antagonism or defensiveness—that's to be expected. At those times, it's clear that badly behaved people are to some degree *unconscious* of the effect they're having in the world—their damaged ego prevents them from seeing what everyone else can plainly see. Some people even demonstrate an awareness of how difficult they can be but selfishly embrace it as *This is who I am—so get over it!*

People who need to exert an influence over Life and the world suffer the most. Ironically, their urgent need to control puts them in positions of power, so while many of society's "leaders" plainly exhibit pain as their inspiration and impetus, our job is to gently but persistently hold the world together with Love.

Immediately recognize that those people are suffering inwardly and outwardly from the challenges of their lives. They feel less-than, victimized, unacknowledged, or singularly justified—all conditions imposed by an ego locked in a powerless prison of how "important" or influential they think they should be. That's when we need to resist simply rejecting them and recognize the pain they're in and the help they may need. It's the time to simply be present with Love in your heart, and open up your authentic self to compassionately accept their expressions of pain. Be of service. Make yourself both an angel and an example, as best you can—and watch what happens. The results will astonish you.

Co-Designing Our Mysteries of Life

At any time, in any life we live, we are occupying a state of our own conscious and unconscious design. Interacting successfully with one another depends on realizing that reality. We emerge into many different worlds when we emerge into this life, and after all of my experiences, for me that has come to mean one thing: that the eternal, authentic me is an *individual* energetic entity created by the information of my being, blending itself into a rich world of multiple dimensions. It stretches out behind me and in front of me. It has been, and still is, my past. It is forming itself now, and will become my future. Through all the Life I've lived, I've been building this expression that I slowly become more and more conscious of as a particular kind of soft-edged quantum "packet" of information—alive in the field of Love and Consciousness—that feathers out, overlapping and combining with the energies of Life. I'm always making choices that will determine what the shape of my life-packet is and will be. The particular individual mission of my purpose grows out of that—the dissolution of all my hard edges and sense of separation—and the same is true for everyone else too.

A big part of our being able to compassionately interact with one another is to recognize and respect our unique positions on our individual tracks of spiritual evolution—and (as if it isn't confusing enough) an even greater challenge comes in trying to comprehend how we blend with one another, and *what our roles are in one another's lives.* That is, why, specifically, are we here for each other? Why have we been drawn together this way?

We're never alone in noticing how synchronistically our lives come together. We all seem to be here, now, to complete one another in a way—to fulfill some unconscious agreement from another lifetime or to lay the groundwork for some transformative experience in our spiritual present or future. Often in this life, we just need to be *right here* for one another (whether we know why or not), with Love in our hearts—no matter what. And maybe to have a few laughs while we do that, please?

In Heaven, relationships are condition-free—all the karma around and between one another is absolutely clear, because the field of Love is absolutely unconditional. Realizing the Love we have between one another makes our true purpose become ever clearer, simply because *it is our true purpose.*

The Most Purposeful Relationships

Obviously, we're meant to be in one another's lives, so as we grow to appreciate how the invisible machinery of this mystery works (on its own eternal schedule), we can presume that there's a good reason for why we find each other when we do. It's either to help one another reach a higher stage of Consciousness through the transformative *alchemy* of Love and then to move on, or to finally remember to forget our own self-centered needs and devote ourselves purely to providing Love and completion to our one person (or "family") for the rest of this life. That way, the ego-self is annihilated in the fire of Love, and we become *soul mates,* bound together in the eternal moment.

With his painfully romantic tongue in cheek, Rumi said, "Everyone chooses a suffering that will change him or her to a well-baked loaf," [33] but why, oh why would we ever mention suffering when we're speaking of love? *Well…*

We meet our soul mate, or get "assigned" to our families, and we intuitively know that we've come together for some secret reason that we're here to discover—but it's not really a secret, is it? It's the realization of Love. Yet, even knowing that won't keep us from behaving in distinctly human ways—developing hurt feelings, petty resentments, even deep splits and "unmendable" rifts between one another—but still, it doesn't change our real purpose one bit. We're still here to love each other unconditionally (if we want to get to Heaven, that is). We must never allow the most profound experience of Love that we're capable of to fall victim to silly ego-mind complaints, such as *What do you mean I look chubby?* or *Why didn't you tell me you talked to my mother earlier?* or even *Why would someone ever fold towels that way?*

In that moment of presence, just stop and say this to yourself: "It makes no difference whether I'm right or wrong about this particularly petty little issue—*I love this person.* What would ever make me want to compromise this divine situation? I love *Love,* and I'm grateful to have it in my life with this amazing person that I've come so far to find, with whom I am inexplicably, inextricably bound together within this eternal ocean of Love."

We all have to concede that we're pretty clueless here. *Love does a transcendent dance around Time and Space to weave our lives together in a critical way with the people we are meant to be with.* These synchronicities are unquestionably the most purposeful relationships in our lives, and there's no way around the complications that come with the ability to experience that kind of Love in this kind of life. It's a kind of chemistry—a catalyst of growth and completion. "The meeting of two personalities is like the contact of two chemical substances: if

---

33. Barks, *The Soul of Rumi,* 25.

there is any reaction, both are transformed," says the good Dr. Jung again.[34]

This transformative quality of relationships—the turbulent alchemy of personal change leading to our wholeness and purpose—is a process of restoring our relationship to our Divine Source by finding that spiritual partner who completes us, what Rumi called *the Friend*, perhaps in the form of *the Lover*. It's the restoration of our two souls as one in the crucible of experience that this life is meant to be. Naturally, in the realization of this kind of spiritual unity, all of our conflicting personal traits will merge—harmoniously or not so harmoniously. All the pairs of opposites that arise in these relationships must come together: joy and sadness, abundance and loss, forceful strength and flexible yielding, independence and reliance, tradition and innovation. In Heaven, the energies that make up this complete profile are aspects within women and men alike—but the characteristics that align us best with a spiritually elevated nature tend to be those we find on the *feminine* side of the spectrum.

Authentic Spiritual Connection through Unified Energy

The characteristics we most often associate with *the Divine Feminine* as being gentle, nurturing, considerate, cooperative, empathetic, emotionally engaged, and intuitive are all characteristics of our more authentic spiritual connection, and demonstrate a natural healthy detachment from the ego-mind. These are the characteristics of Divine Consciousness that prevail in Heaven. In fact, ego-based expressions of forcefulness, domination, and competition don't even exist there, and are also essentially unnecessary and ultimately destructive here on Earth.

I believe that this feminine spiritual ideal is a result of the natural design of our human forms—women are a direct channel to the Divine, a passageway to Source that men will never embody. In this sense, the feminine aspect accesses a naturally ascendant connec-

---

34. Jung, *Modern Man in Search of a Soul*, 49.

tion. When any of us are facing challenges in creating healthy relationships with one another, we all need to be in conscious contact with that ascendant nature of our feminine side. Women who are rightfully conflicted and wrongly oppressed in an often patriarchal world can trust in their heart that the Divine Feminine is reflective to the state of Heaven (in the same sense that the Universe reflects "the Mind of God"). Embracing their feminine nature and being empowered by it is something every world can and will benefit from.

Men, who've come to realize that their unconscious drives are often destructive to the spiritual quality of their lives, need to consciously incorporate the feminine traits that are the source of real extra-dimensional power into their consciousness. Speaking as part of that club, we've got to be more objective about the dangers inherent in expressing our unconscious aspects of masculinity, and consider it in as spiritually nuanced a way as we consider the Divine Feminine. While honoring and encouraging our most positive attributes, proudly and self-confidently erecting "a quality life" is less likely to get you to any experience of Heaven than simply showing up with Love in your heart, being present and supportive, and making yourself of service to others.

The realization of sacred relationships depends on the reunification of our two sides. For our real divine union to take place we have to metaphorically restore our own spark of divinity to wholeness by discovering our own "twin" brother, sister, lover, or Friend—to reunite our gender aspects in the field of Love, so to speak. Then we can find our ideal, authentic self in a kind of balanced fusing of all aspects of our nature, with our most mutually beneficial characteristics on the ascendancy. Our lives can stop being an expression of duality, and become unified by Divine Consciousness.

EXERCISE: *Have an Open-Hearted Day*

As an exercise, spend an open-hearted day of observing others from a spiritual perspective. Engage in a kindly, observant way, and see if you can see people the way angels do—with their insides pouring through whatever surface they're displaying on their outsides. Realize that you do this too, and try to identify as completely as possible with people as you interact with them. It can be a difficult focus to maintain, but it always ends up being really fun and rewarding, and will change your life in some very nice ways by opening up your insides to everybody's outsides, and vice versa.

– 15 –
Create a Divine World:
Making This Place Look More Like Paradise

Potentially, Heaven is spread out wherever you happen to be looking. You can see it in practically every direction you look. It's in the sky and the clouds, in the trees and rivers, and in every inch of Nature. It's in the look in your loved ones' eyes, in the faces of children, in a cat's purr or a dog's wagging tail, and it's even where you might not expect it to be, like in a mailbox or waiting at a bus stop. Life provides us with all of the spiritual elements of Heaven, and this Earth itself provides us with all the material potential that we could ever possibly need. Our Earth is an abundance-making machine, her divine expressions of Life spread out across her beautiful but increasingly troubled face.

Mother Earth, who gently bears us on her surface as we make our giant loop through Time and Space, has always been speaking to us; and if you doubt that, just open your heart, enter this eternal moment, *look* and *listen*. It's impossible not to witness her as a living thing—particularly inasmuch as we are all recipients of the divine generosity she shares with us on her fragile little paradise in space. What more can we do to realize that this really is Heaven, waiting for us to become its citizens?

Choosing Heaven by Returning to a Divine World
The Earth is a dynamic, self-regulating entity that must serve as the source of our inspiration and purpose, although it sometimes seems

that we're taking the long way around to assimilate that reality. There's an extraordinarily rich level of experience awaiting us when we begin to comprehend the real role we're playing in this world.

The wonderfully wise twentieth-century French paleontologist, philosopher, and Jesuit priest, Pierre Teilhard de Chardin, was so far ahead of his time comprehending the interconnectedness of our planet's geological, biological, anthropological, and psycho-spiritual parts, it bothered certain institutions to the point that they prevented the publication of most of his books until after his death. It seems to me that all he was really trying to do was to lead Western civilization back to an ancient spiritual understanding of the life of the Earth—a realization he had first made by simply studying rocks.

Teilhard proposed that following the evolution of the rocky world of inanimate matter and the biological world of reproducing life, a layer of conscious intelligence had emerged, wrapping itself around the surface of the Earth. This layer, which he called the *noosphere,* is composed not only of the evolutionary intelligence of humanity, but also of a dynamic *spiritual* potential, constantly being demonstrated by the emergent capacity for global consciousness, manifesting in all of Life. In his way, he was circling back to the philosophies of our indigenous ancestors, to the living cultures of people who are spiritually aligned with an authentic world and see no lines in Nature between what is or isn't alive—because *everything* is alive. These voices of ancient wisdom lucidly inform us of our true relationship to our planet. As we realize this ourselves, hopefully it won't be too late for us to restore the unifying magic of Heaven to our stricken planet.

With the technological aid of our internet civilization, we've realized a kind of global consciousness already; and as time passes and generations adapt to the everyday instantaneous exchange of ideas and emotions, our shared sixth sense—the reunification of a transpersonal global mind—is blossoming. Personal synchronicities become the same thing as simple coincidences, as there are just too many *connections* joining the course of everyday events. Science keeps finding evidence of deeper levels of intelligence everywhere we look, from discoveries about animal cognition and awareness, to the existence of thousands of other Earth-like planets, to the occupation of mundane objects by artificial intelligence.

Our mass *cognitive dissonance* is cracking apart, and as usual, distress is the agent of transformational change as we awaken to realize the unconscious destruction we've wrought. From out of this corner we've painted ourselves into we can glimpse that illuminative potential (the state of samadhi, bodhi, or gnosis), and like a shifting flock of birds or a darting school of fish, we can change our trajectory very quickly and head back in our truest natural direction. Most likely we are heading that way already, whether we realize it or not.

Beneath it all lies the intuitive understanding of our natural, authentic relationship to our Mother Earth and all the Life that she carries—an ever-evolving expression of a conscious Universe, being eternally expressed. Just like those flocking birds and schooling fish, like subatomic particles and constellating stars, human beings are an inseparable part of it all too. Escaping the ignorance that tells us we're separate and special is how we can start stepping forward into the light. The phenomena of coherence and emergent self-organization aren't confined to waves or planets or particles, or to anthills or to flocks of flamingos—they're real mechanisms of a truly magical and miraculous nature that we are participating in ourselves. Unlike all the other creatures on our planet, we have a defined ability *to choose* the world we want to create for ourselves, a world that impacts all of the other expressions of Consciousness we share this beautiful sphere with.

We are all *psychically, genetically,* and *spiritually* connected with Mother Earth at a fundamental level—at the same level as the birds and fish and ants—but only *we* can choose whether or not to realize the same kind of Heaven on Earth that other creatures know through the nature of their very being. The moment we absorb this reality and open our hearts to the extra-dimensional, non-ordinary, undeniable way we are *one with all Life on the planet,* we'll be on our way to realizing it as the Paradise it was when we were first awakened to find it. We just need to wake up again.

Projecting a Better Path

The natural default of a prehistoric ego-mind is fear, so it's always easy for us to imagine it's the "end of the world," and in our world of change, it is always "the end of the world as we know it," in a way. However, we can actually shape those changes. The shape the world is taking now has been following the collective thoughts we've advanced for some time now, thoughts like *We command all of these earthly elements, The world is too big for us to injure*, and *All of the destructive processes we inflict are reversible*. It only takes a little honesty to know those ideas aren't really true, and that at this rate our ignorance really is destroying the world as we know it. When you're digging yourself into an ever-deepening hole, the first thing to do is to *stop digging*, right?

As human beings, it's easy to expect catastrophes, but from a spiritual perspective, it's easier to see that those scenarios aren't yet real and certainly aren't the only option in a world of infinite variety, evolution, and innovation. Instead of projecting ourselves into inevitable tragedy, we can project intuitively intelligent, spiritual solutions into our future. Thinking with that authentic sanity and then following those thoughts with the right actions allows for new realities to grow. That's how it works in this life. While tremendous change may seem impossible, the reality is that it's happening all the time. In living populations, change isn't a result of what direction the dominant leader goes in, it's because of the shifting realities of each individual; and the instant a majority of the community shifts the same way, the whole community instantly changes direction. This is the shared intuitive intelligence of survival and spiritual evolution.

For me, there's always that one spiritual survival ethic that acts as a very reliable guideline for living, and that's the simple question *Is it Love, or is it Not-Love?*

Seeking the authentic expression of Love in all of the material forms and situations we create in this world is a guaranteed way to create Heaven. Commandments aren't cast down from above; in fact, heavenly solutions and conditions usually start small and grow in a more "grassroots" fashion. Good group direction expands in a horizontal hierarchy that's based on shared perspective, presence, and purpose.

As it is, our world is a pretty complicated place, but *Heaven isn't*— it's just beauty, peace, abundance, Love, understanding, diversity, respect, and so forth. To get that back here, we need to deconstruct *here* a bit, paring down to some basic principles, approaches, and intentions that describe what Heaven on Earth may look like for each of us, and so for all of us together.

We could start by revisiting the Buddha's Eightfold Path (from part II) and consciously practice Right View, Right Purpose, Right Speech, Right Action, Right Vocation, Right Effort, Right Mindfulness, and Right Meditation. It is a proven recipe for good living, since having a spiritual perspective, a recognition of the Sacred, restraint and honesty, benevolence, and generosity of spirit; directing your efforts toward the wellbeing of the life of the planet; maintaining proper concentration and control of your thought processes; and having a consciously aware sense of unity and intuitive intelligence are all you really need. Those are powerful suggestions for leading an ethical, solution-based life that provides us with clear direction.

When in doubt, *be of service* and encourage expressions of spirituality toward all living things, with loving kindness and compassion. When you find like-minded, open-hearted people who are dedicated to the same goals of activism, spiritual evolution, community spirit, and creative expression, join them! If you haven't found a community that does that for you, keep looking or start one yourself (any size group will do). Then all you need to do is simply love your friends, and your friends will love you back.

There is a community of the spirit.
Join it, and feel the delight
of walking in the noisy street, and being the noise …
Close both eyes to see with the other eye.
Open your hands, if you want to be held.
Sit down in this circle.[35]

These suggestions by Rumi do a pretty fair job of describing what Heaven looks like. It's really a grand restoration—circling back to what we know to be beneficial to the greater good. Creating and experiencing Heaven on Earth means embracing what's Love, compassionately restoring what's Not-Love, and celebrating *spiritual common sense!*

Tips for Putting Intuitive Intelligence into Action

A pretty heavenly approach to the stewardship of the planet in an intelligent, commonsense way was intuited by Bill Mollison and David Holmgren, the innovators who conceived of the system known as *permaculture.* Permaculture is a spiritually sensible way of looking at natural systems, and recreating or reproducing them as a balanced approach to sustaining and encouraging Life. It consolidates the basics of the real "intelligent design" the natural world is modeling for us in its patterns and systems, and adopts those intuitively intelligent methods as guiding principles known as the three core tenets of permaculture:

Care for the earth: Provision for all life systems to continue and multiply. This is the first principle, because without a healthy earth, humans cannot flourish.
Care for the people: Provision for people to access those resources necessary for their existence.

Return of surplus: Reinvesting surpluses back into the system to provide for the first two ethics. This includes returning waste back into the system to recycle into usefulness. [36]

These principles of permaculture bring intuitive intelligence into action at every level, starting with each individual bringing them into their own life first. That way, desired results aren't dictated from some top-down pronouncement or promotion, but instead germinate and expand organically into popular approaches based on attraction and functional practicality.

Permaculture is the kind of user-friendly, innovative wisdom that can contribute to a more heavenly life on Earth, directed by honesty, open-mindedness, and the willingness to joyfully leapfrog what isn't working anymore. It's representative of many spiritually superior "alternative" approaches popping up that are based on the common-sense concept of sustainability—honest, evolutionary designs-for-living that require nothing more to set in motion than doing away with our collective ego-based delusions; starting with the idea that what our commercial culture has always told us we needed to be happy isn't what we really need at all. In fact, it's becoming clear that material consumerism is actually a kind of plague that's destroying the beauty and diverse abundance of the Earth. The time is ripe for us to redefine success in ways that empower our spirits and restore our collective soul.

EXERCISE: *Twenty Tips for Living in Heaven*

Realizing the spiritual perspective of Life with honesty and compassion and mindfully connecting ourselves with the causes and effects of our actions with presence makes detachment from the ethical struggles of the world impossible. As with my out-of-body experiences, we just can't put that genie back in the bottle—now we must bring this profound sense of spiritual realism into our actions, based, of course, in the direction of Love. We're not going to change the

---

36. Mollison, *Permaculture: A Designers' Manual,* 2.

world single-handedly, but by expanding our consciousness into Divine Consciousness, we expand our sphere of influence, and within that sphere we can create change. Great leaps in spiritual evolution all come down to the actions of each individual, as a part of the whole. Heaven wasn't built in a day, but in each eternal moment.

Following are twenty tips that I've gleaned over years (of getting smacked on the head). Many have arisen out of a connection with Source and an agenda sincerely created by Love's direction. They are not commandments or guidelines, but tips I follow that might inspire your own personal, purposeful actions based in Love.

1. Celebrate everyone and everything for their *insides* more than their outsides. Recognize that everyone is a reflection of yourself—regardless of any ethnic or cultural differences. Be a witness to your judgments, comparisons, and resentments, and reject them as quickly as you can. Identify with the pain of others, and reflect Love back to them as much as possible. That's Love in action!

2. Love and serve your family, friends, co-workers, and animals unconditionally, knowing them to be your eternal karma partners in the lessons of this life. Purpose yourself to help everyone you love realize all life as expressions of Divine Consciousness.

3. Try not to contribute to the taking of any life—that is Not-Love in its most damaging form. Consider adopting a vegetarian or vegan lifestyle, or take steps in that direction by having "vegetarian days," and by seeking responsible, compassionate sources of protein. Try it for a while, and watch how well it works at every level!

4. Become a preserver and protector of the natural world. The energy of Divine Consciousness is alive in the original forms of Nature, so the faster ego-forms develop and destroy the planet's natural surface, the more hellish the Earth will become.

Celebrate all creatures as direct channels to Love, whose presence is essential for the healing of the planet.

5. Walk or ride a bicycle whenever you can—both are fun and effective ways of contributing to a healthier environment, to your own health, and even to your happiness. Use public transportation—it's efficient and far less destructive, and it allows your spirit to blend with others in the field of shared Consciousness and Love.

6. Engage in and support your community. Get out, get to know everyone you can, and *project kindness*. Take part in door-to-door efforts that create Love-based unity. Patronize your local businesses, and visit them even when you don't need to. Be of service. This plants the energy of Love in the hearts of everyone, which spreads and deepens, connecting entire communities in shared spirituality.

7. Be generous in every way with people who have less, and helpful to those who need help, at any time, expecting nothing in return. Be present for people who are sick or dying the best way you can, as a willing participant in the cycle of Life. Volunteer for good causes. Your contribution of Love in the world will reflect back to you in ways you never imagined.

8. Reuse, repurpose, and recycle everything as much as possible. Try not to waste—actually make an effort to generate *zero* waste. Don't buy uselessly extravagant products or the products of superficial or exploitative industries. Wear good old clothes that are new to you. Reuse furniture, or buy it made from sustainable resources. Carry your own shopping bag. Recycle accumulated surpluses, purging your storage regularly. Reduce your needs to the simplest level of intelligence and practicality. Live lightly and respectfully on the surface of Mother Earth!

9. Eat well, and never too much. Buy fresh food products and organic produce as much as you can. Avoid processed and

packaged food. "Think globally and act locally" by patroniz-
ing local food sources—small, organic producers and farmers'
markets. Where and how you shop can be a form of healthy
activism. Don't overbuy, share your surpluses, and actively
oppose food waste. Avoid chemical additives, artificial ingredients, and genetically modified foods. Celebrate biodiversity
in every way possible. Prepare and share your meals *with Love
as the main ingredient!*

10. Stay away from intoxicants, and—except in carefully admin-
istered cases—from (ameliorative) depressive or stimulating
pharmaceuticals. Not only should their commercial institu-
tional value give you cause for alarm, but the truth is that they
disrupt your spiritual energies and can cause a self-centered
collapse of consciousness *inward,* instead of allowing it to expand. Aside from specifically indicated cases, pharmaceuticals
may not even be necessary, as almost all the healing, comfort, and joy you can imagine are available through essentially
spiritual means. There are naturally based, ritually elemental
psychogenic substances used by indigenous cultures for ages
that can be carefully and responsibly employed to help one
realize the interdimensional depth and connectedness of human life to Consciousness—and to help deal with diagnoses
of terminal disease and the pathological fear of death, for example. Should you choose to try this approach, consult with a
bona-fide expert, and use these substances wisely, sparingly,
and with total respect and care!

11. Be open to "alternative" treatments; often the most effective
approaches are based on natural, traditional, holistic, and ho-
meopathic treatments, traditional energy-balancing therapies,
and common sense. Usually, you already have everything you
need to feel better, and when you learn how to access it—free
of charge—you'll experience a freedom that truly feels like
Heaven.

12. Grow your own garden. If you don't have a yard, grow one in a window box or on a rooftop. Develop a conscious relationship to the plants you grow—they're alive and aware of your energy. Try canning and preserving fresh foods for later enjoyment or for emergencies. Share with your neighbors—growing food is growing Love. In Heaven, Love directs everyone toward self-sufficiency and the potential to provide for others.

13. Conserve energy, and consider converting to clean energy sources, if possible. Become self-sustaining with solar and wind power and reduce your reliance on the energy grid, or augment a reservoir-based power system (and your finances) by returning power back into the system. It's a major effort, but follow the direction of Love away from unsustainable and toxic power sources if you can. True Consciousness will direct us toward limitless clean energy.

14. Interact with technology with as much presence as you can. Media and media-based devices are mind manipulators that cause unnecessary attachments to an ego-based commercial culture. More than in any other part of our modern life, seek *what is Love* and *what is Not-Love*. Engage in the use of technology with the same care as you would with any powerful tool (like a chainsaw). Be present! Engage yourself to accomplish only what you need to for work, family, and community. Detach yourself from emotionally agitating content. Avoid streaming violence and fear-based portrayals of fellow humans as different or dangerous. Our only real solutions are spiritual solutions, so spiritually directed uses of technology for networking and organizing are an important faculty. Use social media to activate Love in your family and extended community. Diligently protect children from damaging content, and balance the effects of technological media with Love. If you suspect that media technology is harming you or your family, *turn it off*. Dispense with it for anything but essential life needs.

15. Reject war, violence, and the weapons culture as completely as possible. In terms of spiritual evolution, these are fear-based expressions that are eternally Not-Love. It's energetically harmful to absorb the energy of hate or violence in any form—don't expose yourself or your loved ones to it if possible.

16. There are no politics in Heaven, but there are civic responsibilities that souls participate in through the choices they make. Do your best to select authentically ethical and moral causes to support. Use civic action to encourage the humane distribution of resources—starting with your community and working outward. Consider being of service yourself.

17. Become honest about the true state of Life on the planet, based in real evidence. Don't get caught up in causes of dominance and control or with persuasive figureheads and agendas—they attach to your ego and promote damaging forms of control, rather than spiritual solutions. *Seek authentic souls* in your leaders, representatives, and social allies, and always analyze political realities through the filter of Love.

18. Engage with your feminine side consciously! For women, this means rejecting the influences of male energy that might make you feel competitive with other women. Fully embrace your own identity as an expression of the Feminine Divine—providing the truest, most reliable channel to Love and to the healing of the planet available to humanity. For men, it means connecting with the power of Love through your innate feminine understanding, and maintaining conscious contact with that aspect. It also means being an example to other, less conscious men by rejecting less harmonious aspects of unconscious male ego, like pride and aggression.

19. Be playful! Enjoy every moment of life and share that joy as much as possible. Forget your ego-based dictates of "right" and "wrong," and practice *tolerance and forgiveness.* Enter into diverse creative undertakings, such as an art project, a musical

group, writing poetry, or dance that expresses your spontaneous physicality. Take part in creative group activities—join a theater or a life-drawing class. Be willing to take risks to bring the energy of expressive co-creation into your life, following Love as it directs you in intuitively creative directions.

20. Surrender into the magical, synchronistic invisible machinery of our interdimensional world, and have faith that it is working in your life, transforming your life in ways that may seem unimaginable. In light of all the evidence, surrendering yourself to what may or may not happen will magically deliver much better results in your life than anything you can plot and plan and attempt to manipulate yourself. Live as authentically as you can, carrying your best skills, talents, and intentions right out in front of you; then just do your best to embody and empower Love, and let go. It really will deliver results that may not be as glamorous or well-timed as you'd like, but are more deeply miraculous than you could ever design for yourself, because they organically allow you to become part of an infinitely greater design.

Hopefully these tips will help you along your way, giving you options and guiding you to detach with Love from needlessly damaging habits, and design a better way of life with compassion, creativity, and respect. Our thoughts and actions can make this world into every expression of beauty it's capable of becoming. Every day, we can contribute to the creation of "Heaven on Earth" here on this very Earth we love by seeking out, following, creating, and embodying material forms of Love as well as we possibly can, and by spiritually aligning ourselves with the unparalleled energies of Love and Divine Consciousness. The deepest wisdom and power that Love can give you lies in the energy you hold in your heart, and how you choose to project it into your world.

Conclusion:
The Everyday Realization
of Heaven

I was born in San Diego, California, and raised in the rocky, red-dust foothills just a few miles from Mexico. The border was porous in those days—you could cross over it back and forth almost as you pleased, so as soon as I was old enough, I'd head south and go exploring, looking mostly for bargains and great Mexican food. Now and then, I'd get lost in the back roads, and have to stop and ask directions.

There might be a very little house there, with a whitewashed fence made out of thin sticks and wire that gave the less-than-modest property a neat and proper look. Barefoot kids were running through the little yard, laughing and stirring up dust. Dad would be home from work, sitting in a chair on the porch. Mom would be heating tortillas, with something good-smelling bubbling in a little pot on an old hot plate.

They were surprised to see me stop and get out of my car, but there were always smiles and gracious gestures, and often they'd offer to share their dinner and a beverage, without any consideration for the obvious scarcity. There was an air of graceful dignity in that little dirt yard, inspired by little more than expressions of Love, everywhere you looked. It was the Love and gratitude that came from having a humble roof overhead, friends and family to laugh with, and enough posolé and tortillas to share with a complete stranger. It was a life of being truly authentic.

It could have been a problem for Dad to provide directions back to the main road, but (there are two kinds of people in the world) usually he'd be happy to put down whatever he was doing and offer to show the way himself.

How Creatively We Paint Our Picture of Heaven

These memories are luminous impressions woven together out of the experiences, the life-data that makes me who I am, pictures that reveal the most important things my life and experiences have taught me. They're examples of Dr. Jung's synchronicity, because their essential truths are framed in my mind and heart by the *meaningful co-incidences* that pop up in my life in one eternal moment after another; the *causal connections* that weave through my life, pulling the parts together like a beautiful script that I could never have written on my own; and the *luminosity*, the divine light that illuminates each event in the vibrant effervescence of Love.

The ability to create your own picture of Heaven grows out of your willingness to escape the constraints of material expectations and consciously co-create a reality well beyond the limitations of our typical lives. It may be nothing like what you've ever imagined—not nearly so grand, or much, much grander. It may look best if you hold it sideways, or turn it upside down. Like the greatest masterpieces yet to be discovered, it's always been a kind of cosmic improvisation.

Your karma is the palette you've always relied on—the colors that come naturally to you, accumulated over lives; the colors you're painting with right now, and some colors you may want to change for tomorrow.

We've already got a "good karma palette" to work from—let's call it the "primary colors of Heaven": kindness, humility, honesty, forgiveness, compassion, and service. Applying these exclusively—in any combination—will always improve our picture in this life-plane. There are more colors available to this palette too—we'll call them *secondary* hues. For example, we mix *humor* in between equal parts of kindness and humility, *self-examination* between humility and honesty, *identifica-*

tion between honesty and forgiveness, *empathy* between forgiveness and compassion, and *generosity* between compassion and service. The generous use of these colors will reflect the luminous, and accurately portray any heavenly atmosphere you wish to depict.

Intention refers to the brushes you use—the tools of manipulating the mysterious muses of your inspiration and creative processes. This is a thoroughly plastic, *quantum* world, where whatever you set the focus of your intention and follow the event stream of your life diligently and with passion, you can manifest out of the potentially material *field of being*. You can make it happen on your canvas if you *believe you can* (with perspective), *show up for it* (with presence), and *keep trying* (with purpose)—just don't hold your brushes too tightly; if you stay relaxed, it's easier to allow other hands to help guide your self-creation.

This is it, as much as I can pass on to you about the way to witness, inhabit, and create this place that we can call Heaven—and to bring along as many other of God's creatures as you possibly can, with Love, of course. You'll find that in these divine surroundings, realized simply by our new perspective, our vigilant dedication to presence, and our clear, coalescing sense of purpose, it really doesn't take much at all to make us truly happy, when before it seemed like it took so very much.

Blessings on your path to discovery, to getting into the beautiful state of being that this Life, and every life, holds in store for all of us. Just remember to always keep the secret password in your open heart, and the password is:

Willingness

Appendix:
Many Heavens to Live, Many Ways to Die: Why We Really (Don't) Die

The title of this book is not without a bit of irony, because whether we actually die and go to Heaven, or can create the experience of Heaven in this life here on this Earth, there is no getting to any form of Heaven without passing through some form of death. You may call it the *metaphor of death and resurrection*—the rising of the mythical Phoenix from the ashes.

One of these days I will die physically, and so will you. As they say, "There's just no getting out of here alive," and though I involuntarily tried it three times already, I'm still afraid of that day—even though I know we don't really die. That instinctual fear of death is part of being human, but don't worry—you can live free, forever, from the threat of obliteration.

Against my will, I purposefully came back from my third NDE to give you some good news and some bad news—based purely on my understanding of it. The good news is that spiritually speaking, we only "die" to this life of flesh and bones and blood, while our spirit continues on; and I can testify to you with great sincerity that as uncomfortable as it may be getting there, the *crossing over* part is a breeze—like instantly stepping out of pain and into a beautiful new life. That is the good news.

The bad news, however, is that *we do have to die*. My late uncle, the great author and philosopher James Hillman, got it right, I think, when he said, "Without a dying to the world of the old order, there is no place for renewal, because…it is illusory to hope that growth is but an additive process requiring neither sacrifice nor death. The soul favors the death experience to usher in change." [37] Our souls do seem to require a death—whether it's an actual death from this life or another form of painful transformation we have to pass through to get to the experience of bliss. In most of our lives, we have to *die in a number of different ways,* none of which are very pleasant and all of which seem designed to accomplish the same thing: to make Heaven more possible. Here's what I mean by that.

If you've ever been around a loved one who's dying, or if you've ever been gravely ill or injured yourself, you know that no claim to fame or fortune remains relevant at all in that grounding bubble of unfortunate reality. What's realized then is a state of absolute humility, where external importance is detached, and there's no pretense of "winning"—even though you really are winning, because you're being *freed.* That's the state where we realize the power of absolute humility, a state of absolute *grace.* In that eternal moment, you're reduced to your most authentic condition of egoless selfhood—free from the expectations and self-imagery you were subjected to for much of your life. You are gracefully, and gratefully reduced to the state of simply being who you are really meant to be.

At that point, you are *I am.*

From that point on, everything becomes possible, because in a cosmically significant way, you're starting over as a free, freshly liberated spirit. In the bigger, trans-dimensional picture, this happens when you actually physically die. That's how to get to Heaven in the Hereafter, but throughout this book I've been talking about getting to Heaven *here on Earth.*

I presume that none of us remember being born, and we usually don't remember how we died, but there are some deaths we probably do remember. So let's look at the other ways, the other "deaths" our souls also seem to require—the "living deaths" that also cause

---

37. Hillman, *Suicide and the Soul,* 68.

us to regenerate ourselves and occupy an unavoidably more authentic life. Let's look at the difficult times that lead us to be "born again" in this life.

All the Ways (and Why) We Experience "Death"

When we've experienced the crushing loss of a family member or dear friend. When a lover or spouse decides to leave us and move on to a new life on their own. When a job or serious expectation we have suddenly, unexpectedly vaporizes. These are all deaths, of a sort, that cause us to reconsider who we thought we were, and to consider anew *who we may have to be from here on.*

Each death of this sort opens up our soul, reveals our authentic self, and causes us to humbly reassess our life. We suddenly become teachable as to how we may need to change and improve our lives on a fundamentally *spiritual* level—freed from the unreliable definitions and expectations of material life that may have ultimately failed to make us feel happy and fulfilled.

Those are *spiritually transformative* eternal moments, when we learn those hardest-of-all lessons—that our material, ego-based outsides can't provide us with what is important: finding Love in this life, and merging back into it.

When we "die" to that superficial sense of ourselves, when we can let go of who we thought we were, we can instantly expand into Divine Consciousness. Suddenly it becomes possible for us to see *who we authentically are*—no longer as separate, searching individuals, but instead as loving, giving, creative, contributing pieces of a Divine Wholeness. In that transformative moment we are reborn as authentic expressions of our infinitely larger Love-based reality. It is the death of our ego and the expansion of our self into our true spiritual potential.

So I'm sorry to say, but happy to announce, that we do have to die to these difficult forms we get stuck in—in what may turn out to be a number of difficult ways. But that's the deal here, this life ain't easy. This *is* a kind of school, and we matriculate from its many different levels by *embracing* our many "little" deaths (and our one "big" one) to liberate us into our unimaginably magical and miraculous potential. Our souls require it to help us find our way to Heaven—in this life, and in every Life.

Bibliography and Interdimensional Reading List

Ambedkar, B. R. *The Buddha and His Dhamma*. Delhi, India: Siddharth Books, 2006.

Arnold, Edwin, trans. *The Song Celestial, or Bhagavad Gita*. New York: Truslove, Hanson, & Comba, Ltd., 1900. http://cincinnatitemple .com/downloads/BhagavadGitaSongCelestial.pdf and www.sacred -texts.com/hin/gita.

Asvaghosa. *The Buddha-Carita*. Translated by E. B. Cowell. New Dehli, Dehli Divine Books, 1977.

Aurobindo, Sri. *Bases of Yoga*. Pondicherry, India: Sri Aurobindo Ashram Trust, 1981.

———. *The Future Evolution of Man*. Pondicherry, India: Sri Aurobindo Ashram Trust, 1963.

———. *Lights on Life-Problems*. Pondicherry, India: Sri Aurobindo Ashram Trust, 1981.

———. *Rebirth and Karma*. Pondicherry, India: Sri Aurobindo Ashram Trust, 1991.

B., Mel. *New Wine*. Center City, MN: Hazelden Foundation, 1991.

Barks, Coleman, trans. *The Essential Rumi*. New York: HarperCollins, 2004.

———. *Rumi: The Book of Love*. New York: HarperCollins, 2003.

———. *The Soul of Rumi*. New York: HarperCollins, 2004.

Besant, Annie, and Bhagavan Das, trans. *The Bhagavad Gita*. London and Benares: Theosophical Publishing Society, 1905. https:// catalog.hathitrust.org/Record/009013723.

Bhikkhu, Anandajoti, ed. and trans. *Dhamma Verses: Dhammapada.* Second edition. 2017. www.ancient-buddhist-texts.net/English -Texts/Dhamma-Verses/Dhamma-Verses.pdf.

Bucke, Richard. *Cosmic Consciousness.* Philadelphia, PA: Innes & Sons, 1901.

Buddharakkhita, Acharya, trans. *The Dhammapada: The Buddha's Path of Wisdom.* Kandy, Sri Lanka: Buddhist Publication Society, 1985. www.buddhanet.net/pdf_file/scrndhamma.pdf.

Burtt, E. A., ed. *The Teachings of the Compassionate Buddha.* New York: New American Library, 1955.

Byrom, Thomas, trans. *Dhammapada: The Sayings of the Buddha.* Boston, MA: Shambhala Publications, 1993.

Campbell, Joseph. *A Joseph Campbell Companion.* Edited by Diane K. Osbon. New York: HarperCollins, 1991.

Chödrön, Pema. *When Things Fall Apart: Heart Advice for Difficult Times.* Boston, MA: Shambhala Publications, 1997.

Dalai Lama, HH [Tenzin Gyatso]. *How to Practice: The Way to a Meaningful Life.* Translated and edited by Jeffrey Hopkins. New York: Pocket Books, 2002.

Dalai Lama, HH [Tenzin Gyatso], and Howard Cutler. *The Art of Happiness: A Handbook for Living.* New York: Riverhead Books, 1998.

Dyer, Wayne W. *Everyday Wisdom.* Carlsbad, CA: Hay House, 2005.

———. *Real Magic: Creating Miracles in Everyday Life.* New York: HarperCollins, 1992.

———. *Your Sacred Self: Making the Decision to Be Free.* New York: HarperCollins, 1995.

Easwaran, Eknath, trans. *The Bhagavad Gita.* Tomales, CA: The Blue Mountain Center of Meditation/Nilgiri Press, 1985 and 2007.

———. *The Dhammapada.* Tomales, CA: The Blue Mountain Center of Meditation/Nilgiri Press, 1985.

Eliot, T. S. *Selected Essays.* New York: Harcourt, Brace & Co. 1932.

Gallup, George Jr., with William Proctor. *Adventures in Immortality.* New York: McGraw-Hill, 1982.

Gandhi, Mohandas K. *The Bhagavad Gita According to Gandhi*. Blacksburg, VA: Wilder Publications, 2011.

———. *The Way to God*. Berkeley, CA: Berkeley Hills Books, 1999.

Harvey, Andrew, ed. *The Essential Mystics: Selections from the World's Great Wisdom Traditions*. San Francisco, CA: HarperCollins, 1996.

Hillman, James. *Philosophical Intimations*. Edited by Edward S. Casey. Thomson, CT: Spring Publications, 2016.

———. *Suicide and the Soul*. New York: Harper & Row, 1964.

Hoeller, Stephan A. *Gnosticism: New Light on the Ancient Tradition of Inner Knowing*. Wheaton, IL: Quest Books, 2002.

———. *Jung and the Lost Gospels: Insights into the Dead Sea Scrolls and the Nag Hammadi Library*. Wheaton, IL: Theosophical Publishing House, 1989.

Huxley, Aldous. *The Perennial Philosophy*. New York: Harper & Brothers, 1945.

Jacobs, Alan, ed. and trans. *The Gnostic Gospels*. London, UK: Duncan Baird Publishers, 2005.

James, William. *Varieties of Religious Experience*. New York: The Modern Library, 1936.

Jung, C. G. *Memories, Dreams, Reflections*. New York: Random House, 1961.

———. *Modern Man in Search of a Soul*. New York: Harcourt, 1955.

———. *Synchronicity: An Acausal Connecting Principle*. Princeton, NJ: Princeton University Press, 1969.

Kalu Rinpoche, Kyabje Dorje Chang. *The Dharma That Illuminates All Beings Like the Light of the Sun and the Moon*. Albany, NY: State University of New York Press, 1986.

Knoblauch, Hubert, Ina Schmied, and Bernt Schnettler. "Different Kinds of Near-Death Experience: A Report on a Survey of Near-Death Experiences in Germany." *Journal of Near-Death Studies* 20, no. 1 (September 2001).

Kongtrul, Jamgon. *The Great Path of Awakening*. Boston, MA: Shambhala Publications, 1987.

Lambdin, Thomas O., trans. *The Gospel of Thomas*. Claremont, CA: The Gnostic Society, 1974.

Lao Tzu. *Tao Te Ching*. Translated by Jonathan Star. New York: Jeremy P. Tarcher/Putnam, 2001.

———. *Tao Te Ching*. Translated by Stephen Mitchell. New York: Harper & Row, 1988.

Laszlo, Ervin. *Quantum Shift in the Global Brain: How the New Scientific Reality Can Change Us and Our World*. Rochester. VT: Inner Traditions, 2008.

———. *Science and the Akashic Field: An Integral Theory of Everything*. Rochester, VT: Inner Traditions, 2004.

Leloup, Jean-Yves, trans. *The Gospel of Thomas: The Gnostic Wisdom of Jesus*. Rochester, VT: Inner Traditions, 2005.

Manitara, Olivier. *The Essenes: From Jesus to Our Time*. Montreal, Canada: Telesma-Evida Publishing, 1998.

Mascaro, Juan, trans. *The Upanishads*. Middlesex, UK: Penguin Books, 1965.

McTaggart, Lynne. *The Field: The Quest for the Secret Force of the Universe*. New York: HarperCollins, 2008.

Mehrotra, Rajiv. *All You Ever Wanted to Know from His Holiness the Dalai Lama on Happiness, Life, Living, and Much More*. Carlsbad, CA: Hay House, 2009.

Miller, Ron. *The Gospel of Thomas: A Guidebook for Spiritual Practice*. Woodstock, VT: SkyLight Paths, 2004.

Mollison, Bill. *Permaculture: A Designers' Manual*. Tyalgum, Australia: Tagari Publications, 1988.

Montaigne, Michel de. *Essais*. Translated by Charles Cotton. 1877. www.gutenberg.org/files/3600/3600-h/3600-h.htm.

Müller, F. Max, trans. *The Dhammapada*. Oxford: Clarendon Press, 1881. www.sacred-texts.com/bud/sbe10/index.htm.

Natarajan, A. R., ed. *A Practical Guide to Know Yourself: Conversations with Sri Ramana Maharshi*. Bangalore, India: Ramana Maharshi Centre for Living, 2002.

Nhat Hanh, Thich. *You Are Here: Discovering the Magic of the Present Moment.* Boston, MA: Shambhala Publications, 2009.

Nisargadatta, Maharaj. *Consciousness and the Absolute.* Edited by Jean Dunn. Durham, NC: Acorn Press, 1994.

———. *I Am That.* Durham, NC: Acorn Press, 1988.

Prabhavananda, Swami, and Christopher Isherwood, trans. *Bhagavad-Gita: The Song of God.* Introduction by Aldous Huxley. New York: New American Library, 2002.

———. *How to Know God: The Yoga Aphorisms of Patanjali.* Hollywood, CA: Vedanta Press, 1981.

———. *Shankara's Crest-Jewel of Discrimination: Timeless Teachings on Nonduality.* Hollywood, CA: Vedanta Press, 1975.

Robinson, James M., ed. *The Nag Hammadi Library.* New York: Harper & Row, 1988.

Sargeant, Winthrop, trans. *The Bhagavad Gita.* Albany, NY: State University of New York Press, 2009.

Schoedel, W. R., trans. *The Gospel of Thomas.* Leiden, Holland: The Brill Edition. www.reluctant-messenger.com/gospel-thomas -Messrs-Brill_of_Leiden.htm.

Smedes, Lewis B. "Forgiveness: The Power to Change the Past." *Christianity Today* (January 7, 1983). www.christianitytoday.com /ct/2002/decemberweb-only/12-16-55.0.html.

Suzuki, Shunryu. *Zen Mind, Beginner's Mind.* New York: Walker/ Weatherhilll, 1970.

Thurman, Robert. *Infinite Life: Awakening to Bliss Within.* New York: Berkley Publishing Group/Riverhead Books, 2004.

Trungpa, Chögyam. *Meditation in Action.* Boston, MA: Shambhala Publications, 1969.

van Lommel, P., R. van Wees, V. Meyers, and I. Elfferich. "Near-Death Experience in Survivors of Cardiac Arrest: A Prospective Study in the Netherlands." *Lancet* 358, no. 9298 (December 15, 2001).

Walsh, Roger. *Essential Spirituality.* New York: J. Wiley, 1999.

White Eagle. *The Quiet Mind*. New Lands, UK: White Eagle Publishing Trust, 1972.

Williamson, Marianne. *Illuminata: A Return to Prayer*. New York: Riverhead Books, 1995.

Acknowledgments

My very deepest thanks to all the teachers of light who've helped me become a grateful celebrant of this and every life we live. It's a long list that for me will always include His Holiness the Dalai Lama, Eknath Easwaran, Joseph Campbell (and Bill Moyers), Sri Aurobindo, C. G. Jung, Swami Prabhavananda and Christopher Isherwood, Marianne Williamson (many Tuesdays), Robert Thurman, William Wilson, Shunryu Suzuki Roshi, Ernst Laszlo, and the late, great Wayne Dyer. There are so many others—just too many to mention.

A very special thanks to the very gracious Coleman Barks for the remarkable work of his life, and for permission to use his beautiful translations of the poetry of Rumi.

The guiding lights of this effort have been my literary sage, Doris Grumbach, my late uncle, James Hillman, and my ideals of the voice on the page, Martin Rowe, Lewis Lapham, Kurt Vonnegut, and Caroline Pincus—thank you for making my writing life possible. Special thanks to Bryan Connelly at Gaia.com, Kiva Bottero at The Mindful Word.org, Patty Malek at Soul Life Times.com, Victor Fuhrman, Michael Neeley, and many others for giving my ideas and experiences a stage online and on the air, and for all of the nice folks who visit and read my blog and follow along on social media.

My most practical thanks of all go to my friend and agent Tom Miller at the Carol Mann Agency, and to my editors at Llewellyn: Angela Wix, for her patient guidance and quest for the best, and Andrea Neff, for helping me to think better.

Thank you to my spiritual mentors Raymond Lewis, Brother Edward Salisbury, Bukai Dainin Thomas Ingalls of the San Francisco Zen Center, Don Weller, and Rich Masterson. A special thank you to Pandit Rajmani Tigunait for lunch, books, and much more at the Tibetan Institute; to Amma; and to Professor Barry Horlor, for making me a seeker. To mentors recently passed and very much missed: Phil Parker, Saul Lambert, Harry Feitelson, David Johnson, Beth Young, and Gary Gaynor. Thanks to my spiritual supporters, sounding boards, and creative encouragement Cha Cha Weller, George Nelson, Margot McLean,

Jerilyn Hesse, Michael Goldbarg, Franz Schalk, Suzanne Martikas, James Trotta-Bono, and Rena Dunsworth. For my annual family Petrula Vrontikis, Glenn Martinez, Barbara Kuhr and John Plunkett, Wayne Hunt, Francois Robert, and Jane Gittings, with endless love.

To Linda Truax, Chuck Swedrock, Susan Amsden, and Lee Witting, of the International Association for Near Death Studies for the work they do, and their role in helping my voice to be heard.

And most of all, to the Feminine Divine in my life, my beautiful wife, Sue; my mother, Dorothy; Anne, my guardian angel; Sybil Pike; Ruth, Margaret, and Pamela Moffett. To all my angels and ancestors, and my eternal brother in Heaven, Maxwell—*hermano de mi corazón*.

Always with Love.

Index

A

affinity bias, 141

afterlife, 1–3, 12, 25, 88, 150

ahimsa, 72, 173

Akasha, 49, 132

Akashic records, 49, 132

alchemy, alchemical, 59, 100, 190, 192

Alcoholics Anonymous, 186

amygdala, 139

analytical meditation, 157, 158, 162

anchor bias, 141

ancient wisdom, 98, 114, 196

angels, 16, 17, 25, 59, 65, 66, 68, 78, 92, 130, 134, 157, 159, 160, 163, 164, 173, 185, 187–189, 193, 224

anger, 7, 23, 58, 59, 108, 114, 164

animals, 17, 28, 70, 71, 138, 143, 175–178, 202

annihilation, 122, 161, 174

archetypes, 95

architecture, 4, 5, 11, 36, 119, 136, 147

Arjuna, 104–106

art, 63, 68, 119, 147, 148, 154, 206

atman, 105, 115, 132

attachments, 20, 21, 123, 142, 144, 205

Aurobindo, Sri, 165, 217, 223

authentic self, 18–20, 67, 108, 115, 123, 130, 138, 159, 185, 189, 193, 215

Avalokiteshvara, 161

B

Barks, Coleman, 86, 106, 120–123, 191, 200
Bhagavad Gita, 99, 104, 106–109, 119, 156, 217–219, 221
bias
 affinity, 141
 anchor, 9, 141
 confirmation, 141, 144
 in-group/out-group, 140
Black Elk Speaks, 125
bliss, 3, 10, 110, 111, 121, 124, 169, 214
bodhi, 111, 114, 159, 168, 197
bodhicitta, 146
Brahman, 105, 106, 119
Buddha, 11, 30, 88, 98, 99, 109, 110, 112, 114, 116, 119, 153, 160, 161, 164, 166–168, 199, 217, 218
Buddhism, 42, 72, 109, 116, 133, 146

C

Campbell, Joseph, 88, 132, 218, 223
Chandogya Upanishad, 125
Christhood, 166
Cloud of Unknowing, The, 99
cognitive dissonance, 144, 149, 154, 176, 178, 197
community, 44, 58, 83, 84, 121, 198–200, 203, 205, 206
confirmation bias, 141, 144
connections, 96, 99, 142, 196, 210
constraint, 90
consumerism, 180, 201
Course in Miracles, A, 88
Creation, 37, 56, 105, 137, 162, 175, 207
creativity, 154, 175, 207
Crest Jewel of Discrimination (Shankara's), 99, 125

D

data, 29, 49, 85, 87, 93, 106, 132, 136, 154

Dalai Lama, the 14th, 63, 68, 218, 220, 223

death, 1, 4, 5, 35, 40, 49, 70, 76, 85, 92, 95, 97, 103, 111, 127, 164, 168, 171, 172, 196, 204, 213–215

denial, 50, 53, 72, 145, 149, 177

dervish, 121, 122

Descartes, René, 153

devotional meditation, 160, 163

Dhammapada, 99, 113, 114, 119, 156, 164, 218, 220

dharma, 106

Dickinson, Emily, 120, 125

difficult people, 188

dimensions, 189

discomfort, 58, 78, 84, 145

Divine, the, 21, 30, 71, 72, 78, 79, 88, 92, 100, 105, 106, 108, 115, 122, 124, 127, 132, 137, 142, 143, 150, 161, 169, 171, 172, 174–176, 178, 181, 182, 186, 192, 193, 195, 210

Divine Consciousness, 3, 5, 12, 18, 21, 93, 100, 105, 137, 144, 149, 161, 186, 187, 192, 193, 202, 207, 215

Divine Feminine, 192, 193

duality, 15, 21, 100, 155, 193

Dyer, Wayne, 88, 141, 218, 223

dying, 5, 134, 203, 214

E

Earth, 4, 11, 13, 19, 21, 27, 32, 65, 69, 70, 72, 77, 81, 97, 100, 105, 118, 143, 149, 150, 153, 162, 167, 168, 171, 174–176, 178, 179, 192, 195–197, 199–203, 207, 213, 214

ecstatic, ecstasy, 119, 120, 122, 123

ego annihilation, 122, 133, 161, 174, 190

ego-mind, 16, 19, 20, 50, 51, 66, 67, 72–74, 78, 90, 100,
    123, 140, 166, 175, 182, 185–187, 191, 192, 198
ego-self, 22, 68, 133, 166, 174, 190
ego-voice, 17, 18, 51
Eightfold Path, 110, 112, 113, 199
Eliot, T. S., 119, 218
energy, 5, 6, 11, 23, 25, 27–30, 39, 44, 64, 67, 76, 80,
    82–84, 92, 94, 96, 100–102, 113, 121, 125, 129, 135,
    147, 148, 150, 161, 163, 172, 174–179, 182, 183, 188,
    192, 202, 203, 205–207
Eternal, the, 5, 28, 47, 66, 85, 88, 89, 93, 96, 97, 100,
    101, 106, 108, 111, 117, 125, 132, 133, 143, 146, 155,
    159–161, 165, 168, 174, 189, 190
eternal moment, the, 5, 28, 66, 85, 88, 89, 93, 96, 97,
    100, 125, 155, 159–161, 165, 168, 174, 190

F
fana, 159
fear, 7, 17, 23, 131, 133, 139, 164, 168, 177, 183, 198,
    204, 213
food, 27, 147, 148, 174, 175, 203–205, 209
forgiveness, 10, 22, 23, 55–60, 63, 82, 89, 90, 106, 118,
    119, 124, 149, 172, 184, 185, 188, 206, 210, 211
Four Noble Truths, 109, 110, 112
Franklin, Benjamin, 49
Fullness, the, 119

G
Gandhi, Mahatma, 44, 72, 160, 173, 219
Gita, the, 99, 104–109, 119, 156, 217–219, 221
Gnosticism, Gnostic, 13, 99, 114–120, 219, 220
gnosis, 114–118, 159, 197
God, 3, 4, 15, 105, 106, 131, 132, 140, 160, 193, 211,
    219, 221

Gospel of John, 99
Gospel of Thomas, 13, 99, 116–119, 220, 221
Great Spirit, the, 71, 176
Gyatso, Tenzin (the Dalai Lama), 63, 218

H
happiness, 4, 10, 12, 37, 40, 41, 44, 55, 57, 63, 64, 68,
    104, 110, 111, 113, 114, 117, 136, 139, 146, 154, 165,
    166, 203
Heinlein, Robert, 67
hell, 4, 5, 8, 15, 16, 35, 48, 153, 186
Hermetica, 125
Hillman, James, 213, 214, 219, 223
Hinduism, Hindu, 10, 18, 72, 99, 104, 119, 132, 148
Holmgren, David, 200
honesty, 10, 22, 23, 42, 47–53, 55, 60, 82, 90, 106, 118,
    119, 124, 144, 149, 172, 184, 198, 199, 201, 210, 211
humiliation, 35, 48
humility, 10, 22, 23, 35, 37–44, 48, 51, 55, 65, 76, 77, 81,
    90, 106, 118, 119, 124, 132, 144, 149, 172, 184, 210,
    214

I
Illuminata, 97, 222
illumination, Divine Illumination, 92, 96, 102, 146,
    159
imagination, 5, 7, 18, 23, 67, 72–74, 91, 109, 133, 163
impermanence, 107, 111, 112, 119
in-group/out-group bias, 140
individuation, 95
intention, 71, 77, 86, 89, 91, 94, 108, 112, 130, 132, 147,
    150, 162, 181, 184, 211
interdependence, 111, 119, 176
intuition, 44, 54, 151, 164, 174

intuitive intelligence, 11, 21, 37, 50, 51, 54, 90, 155, 163,
    173, 177, 185, 198–201

J
Jainism, 173
James, William, 99
Jesus, 98, 160, 161, 166, 167, 220
Jung, Carl G., 88, 95, 96, 183, 192, 210, 219, 223

K
Kant, Immanuel, 88, 127
karma, 49, 53, 91, 105, 106, 124, 130–132, 136, 137,
    144, 167, 172, 188, 190, 202, 210, 217
karma yoga, 105
kindness, 10, 22, 23, 25–33, 38, 43, 49, 55, 71, 81, 90,
    106, 112, 114, 118, 119, 124, 140, 144, 149, 162, 172,
    183, 184, 199, 203, 210
koan (Zen), 116–117

L
ladder (to Heaven), 23, 68
Lao Tzu, 36, 99, 220
Lascaux, 147
Luke, 32, 167
luminosity, luminous, 59, 68, 94, 96, 97, 105, 111, 114,
    117, 182, 210, 211
lust, 59, 108

M
magic, magical, 1, 2, 11, 18, 21, 28, 69, 80, 81, 91, 94,
    117, 119, 120, 152, 157, 162, 196, 197, 207, 216
Mahabarata, 104
Maharshi, Ramana, 143, 220
Mandela, Nelson, 44

mantra, 161
Mara, 166–168
matrix, 38, 49, 88, 115, 117, 149, 160
meditation
    analytical, 157, 158, 162
    devotional, 160, 163
    goals of, 155–156
    physical, 105, 161, 163
    self-guided, 169
    tonglen, 162
Mexico, 209
mindfulness, 89, 111, 113, 199
moksha, 105
Mollison, Bill, 200, 201, 220
Montaigne, Michel de, 42, 220
Mother Earth, 195, 197, 203
Mother Teresa, 44
mythology, 10, 95, 115

N
Near Death Experience(s), 1–8, 21, 35, 47, 49, 76, 85, 92,
    95, 97, 98, 103, 114, 127, 129, 151, 164, 165, 213
Neruda, Pablo, 120
New Testament, 92
nirvana, 88, 109, 111, 157, 164
noosphere, 196

O
obliteration, 213

P
pain, 16, 31, 40, 50, 56–59, 64, 70, 72, 81, 112–114, 122,
    124, 125, 144–146, 153, 157, 162, 166, 172, 183–185,
    189, 202, 213

pantheism, 172
Paradise, 9, 12, 55, 72, 88, 121, 125, 195, 198
paranormal(ity), 149, 150
Patanjali, 99, 125, 132, 221
pathology, 145
Perennial Philosophy, The, 100, 219
permaculture, 200, 201, 220
Phaedrus, 99
pharmaceuticals, 204
physical meditation, 105, 161, 163
Pirkei Avot, 99, 125
Plato, 88, 99
play, playfulness, 2, 10, 36, 66, 85, 107, 137, 138, 149,
    150, 154, 157, 158, 175
pleroma, 115
pneuma, 115
poetry, 11, 99, 103, 119–122, 125, 147, 206, 223
prayer, 58, 59, 92, 97, 101, 161, 164, 186
prehistoric, 139, 153, 155, 182, 184, 198
presence, 2, 6–11, 21, 35, 65, 68, 85–93, 95–98, 100–104,
    108, 111, 113, 117, 119–122, 125, 133, 135, 147, 155,
    160, 161, 165, 166, 168, 171, 173, 187, 188, 191, 199,
    201, 202, 205, 211
projection, projecting, 31, 66, 183, 188, 198
Psalms, 125
psychology, 51

Q
Quakers, 163

R
radiance, 92, 114, 119, 120, 148, 168
reaction, overreacting, 7, 54, 59, 80, 90, 192
recycling, 203

resentment, 60

restoration, 132, 179, 186, 192, 200

Rilke, Rainer Maria, 120

Rumi, Jalal ad-Din Muhammad, 11, 23, 86, 99, 106, 119–125, 133, 191, 192, 200

S

Sacred, the, 161, 171, 173–180, 199

sadness, 60, 69–72, 145, 149, 154, 192

sakshi, 18, 20, 57, 148

sama, 122

samadhi, 105, 114, 159, 197

Sanskrit, 18, 86, 132

Satan, 166

Schrödinger, Erwin, 88

selfishness, 55, 146

selflessness, 146

Serlingpa, Lord, 146

Sermon on the Mount, The, 125

Shankara, 99, 221

Shams of Tabriz, 122

sixth sense, sixth-sensory, 19, 44, 69, 96, 174, 176, 178, 196

Smedes, Lewis B., 57, 221

Smith, Dr. Bob, 186

Socrates, 88, 98

Source, the, 15, 28, 37, 49–53, 58, 64, 72, 88, 89, 106, 108, 145, 146, 148, 166, 193, 195

space, 15, 16, 29, 67, 102, 152, 155, 159, 161, 162, 165, 171, 187, 191, 195

spiritual machinery, 105

spiritual transformation, 116

Star Wars, 165, 173

stewardship, 71, 136, 175, 176, 200

(the) still, small voice, 54, 163, 173

Stranger in a Strange Land, 67

Sufism, Sufi, 120, 121, ii

suffering, 31, 58, 82, 109–113, 115, 134, 140, 145, 146, 153, 162, 166, 173, 189, 191

surrender, 11, 36, 98, 102, 120, 123, 124, 129, 137, 146, 163, 167, 185, 186, 207

synchronicity, 94–96, 177, 210, 219

T

Tagore, Rabindranath, 125

Tao Te Ching, 36, 99, 125, 220

Taoism, 36

technology, 7, 52, 97, 99, 205

Teilhard de Chardin, Pierre, 196

television, TV, 98, 99, 132, 152

Thoreau, Henry David, 85

Tibet, 63

Tolle, Eckhart, 88

tonglen, 162

U

Unified Consciousness, 108, 159, 163, 174, 186

unus mundus, 96

V

Varieties of Religious Experience, The, 99, 219

Vedas, 88, 106

vegetarianism, vegan, 178, 202

violence, 108, 180, 205

W

Watts, Alan, 88

Wenders, Wim, 65

Whitman, Walt, 99, 125
Williamson, Marianne, 88, 97, 222, 223
Wilson, Bill, 186, 223
Wings of Desire, 65

Y
Yeshua, 117
yoga
 bhakti, 105
 hatha, 105
 karma, 105
 raja, 105
Yoga Sutras, 99, 125, 132

Z
Zen, 42, 116, 117, 221, 223

To Write to the Author

If you wish to contact the author or would like more information about this book, please write to the author in care of Llewellyn Worldwide Ltd. and we will forward your request. Both the author and the publisher appreciate hearing from you and learning of your enjoyment of this book and how it has helped you. Llewellyn Worldwide Ltd. cannot guarantee that every letter written to the author can be answered, but all will be forwarded. Please write to:

Robert Kopecky
℅ Llewellyn Worldwide
2143 Wooddale Drive
Woodbury, MN 55125-2989

Please enclose a self-addressed stamped envelope for reply,
or $1.00 to cover costs. If outside the U.S.A., enclose
an international postal reply coupon.

Many of Llewellyn's authors have websites with additional information and resources. For more information, please visit our website at www.llewellyn.com.

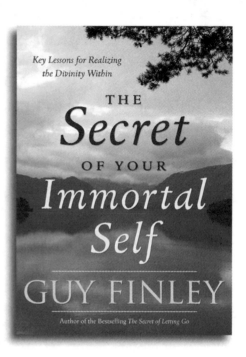

Key Lessons for Realizing
the Divinity Within

THE
Secret
OF YOUR
Immortal
Self

GUY FINLEY

Author of the Bestselling *The Secret of Letting Go*

The Secret of Your Immortal Self
Key Lessons for Realizing the Divinity Within
GUY FINLEY

Open the doors to self-understanding and let go of suffering. Guy Finley helps you seek a deeper relationship with the Divine and provides powerful insights on how to find a guiding light in any dark moment.

Filled with unique and meaningful essays, this guide helps you remember a long-forgotten part of your true, timeless nature. This recollection stirs the sleeping soul that, once awakened, leads you to the crowning moment of life: contact with the immortal Self. Once achieved, this celestial union releases you from imagined self-limitation and regret, granting you the realization that death is not the end of life.

978-0-7387-4407-0, 368 pp., 5 x 7   **$16.99**

BRIDGET BENSON

WE WALK
BESIDE YOU
ALWAYS

Comforting messages from your
loved ones in the afterlife

We Walk Beside You Always
Comforting Messages from Your Loved Ones in the Afterlife
BRIDGET BENSON

Your family and friends in spirit are only a thought away, ready to provide hope and healing throughout your life. They can hear you talk to them, offer practical advice from the afterlife, and help you move past grief. With warmth and honesty, Irish medium Bridget Benson shares uplifting true stories of the ways in which our passed-on loved ones are still very much involved in our lives.

We Walk Beside You Always presents remarkable, first-hand communication between Bridget and those from the other side. Each story is taken from her own experiences and her lifetime spent helping others connect with spirit. Explore the afterlife accounts of children, beloved companion animals, and those who have taken their own life. Discover Bridget's deep connections with her family members in spirit and her near-death experience. With this book, you'll realize life is eternal and the ones you've lost are not gone ... they are always with you.

978-0-7387-3749-2, 240 pp., 5 ³⁄₁₆ x 8   **$14.99**

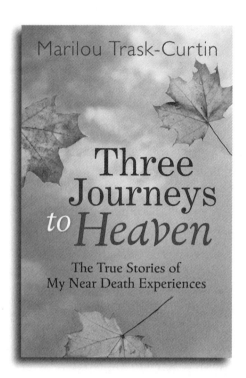

Marilou Trask-Curtin

Three Journeys to Heaven

The True Stories of
My Near Death Experiences

Three Journeys to Heaven
The True Stories of My Near Death Experiences
Marilou Trask-Curtin

Three Journeys to Heaven is the remarkable story of Marilou Trask-Curtin's miraculous near death experiences. Gifted with many psychic talents, visionary dreams, and the ability to explore past lives in regression sessions, Marilou is unique in that she has experienced three near death experiences starting when she was just three years old. In this book she will take us through the basics of near death experiences and then describe in detail what happened during all three of her encounters and how each impacted her amazing life.

978-0-7387-4132-1, 264 pp., 5 ³⁄₁₆ x 8   **$15.99**

To order, call 1-877-NEW-WRLD or visit llewellyn.com
Prices subject to change without notice

The True Story
of a Mother's Reconnection
with Her Son in the Hereafter

By
ℳORNING'S ℒIGHT

GINNY BROCK
Foreword by Patrick Mathews

By Morning's Light
The True Story of a Mother's Reconnection with her Son in the Hereafter
Ginny Brock

Nothing could have prepared Ginny Brock for the most devastating experience a parent can have—the death of her child. But after an amazing vision in which she finds herself guiding her son Drew's spirit into the light, Ginny embarks on a journey that teaches her that our lost loved ones can, in fact, remain very present in our lives.

From vivid dreams to meaningful signs, Ginny learns to recognize how those in spirit communicate with their loved ones on earth. This remarkable true story recounts the beautiful messages Ginny received from the other side, and the extraordinary one-on-one conversations she continues to have with her son Drew.

By Morning's Light offers hope to anyone who has ever lost a loved one, showing how we can indeed move through profound grief and continue to have a relationship with those we love.

978-0-7387-3294-7, 336 pp., 5 ³⁄₁₆ x 8   **$15.95**

To order, call 1-877-NEW-WRLD or visit llewellyn.com
Prices subject to change without notice

OVER 100,000 COPIES SOLD!

MICHAEL NEWTON, PH.D.

DESTINY
OF
SOULS

NEW CASE STUDIES OF
LIFE BETWEEN LIVES

Destiny of Souls
New Case Studies of Life Between Lives
MICHAEL NEWTON

A pioneer in uncovering the secrets of life, internationally recognized spiritual hypnotherapist Dr. Michael Newton takes you once again into the heart of the spirit world. His groundbreaking research was first published in the bestselling *Journey of Souls*, the definitive study on the afterlife. Now, in *Destiny of Souls*, the saga continues with 70 case histories of real people who were regressed into their lives between lives. Dr. Newton answers the requests of the thousands of readers of the first book who wanted more details about various aspects of life on the other side. *Destiny of Souls* is also designed for the enjoyment of first-time readers who haven't read *Journey of Souls*.

Explore the meaning behind your own spiritual memories as you read the stories of people in deep hypnosis, and learn fascinating details about:

—Our purpose on Earth
—Soul mates and spirit guides
—Spiritual settings and where souls go after death
—Soul travel between lives
—Ways spirits connect with and comfort the living
—The soul-brain connection
—Why we choose certain bodies

978-1-56718-499-0, 432 pp., 6 x 9   **$18.99**

To order, call 1-877-NEW-WRLD or visit llewellyn.com
Prices subject to change without notice

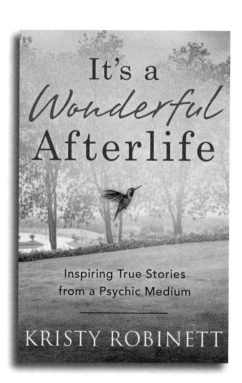

It's a Wonderful Afterlife

Inspiring True Stories
from a Psychic Medium

KRISTY ROBINETT

It's a Wonderful Afterlife
Inspiring True Stories from a Psychic Medium
KRISTY ROBINETT

Ever since she was a child, psychic medium Kristy Robinett has communicated with spirits who have shared their experiences of death and what happens afterwards. In this collection of heartwarming stories that answer the most common questions about the afterlife, Robinett delves into the nature of heaven, if there is a hell, and what the transition to the Other Side is like. With personal experiences and stories from clients, Kristy explores the many signs and symbols that our loved ones share with us to assure that it is, indeed, a wonderful afterlife.

978-0-7387-4073-7, 240 pp., 5 ³⁄₁₆ x 8   **$15.99**